<u>Healing the Wound That Won't Heal</u>
The Reality of Trauma

Jo Spencer

ISBN-13: 978-1523601448
ISBN-10: 1523601442

I dedicate this book to my children; for all the times and all the ways I wasn't there.

And, to my infant self. I heard you crying deep within my heart and promised I will always be here to listen.

CONTENTS

Prologue

This book was first published sixteen years ago. At that time, I had worked as a counselor in the mental health field for twenty years. Then, the incidents that I write about in this introduction forced me to begin looking into the neglect and abandonment trauma I suffered during the first year of my life. Since then, I have never wavered in my commitment to understand myself, and to increase awareness about early trauma and its consequences, psychologically and biologically.

What I have encountered in my quest to be a trauma educator has been one obstacle after another. We have a very deep neurosis in how we view what trauma is. Because post-traumatic stress is so wide-spread and on-going, anyone who endeavors to work with suffering humans needs to have some understanding of what psychological trauma is, how it endures over time, what it does to the brain, body, mind and soul of its victim. And then, of course, to work to ameliorate the suffering.

My own particular 'case' holds much that should be of interest to anyone studying trauma; an infancy shared with my father in his post-World War II deterioration and death, then a childhood that was otherwise non-traumatic, a twenty-year career in the mental health field and a concurrent dedication to psychology, and then the absolute realization that all the emotional problems I had repressed and hidden for a lifetime were rooted right back there in a one-room apartment with my parents in Middletown, Ohio.

Because my neglect and trauma was pre-cognitive, occurring before I had words and mental constructs, before conscious memories could even be formed or repressed, the work I do inwardly is not the same as someone, who, for instance, is uncovering and attempting to heal traumas that happened in childhood and after. By *digging my way out* I have unearthed valuable clues and evidence as to what trauma is and how it gets woven into the fibers of our being.

In the first paragraph of this introduction I use the analogy of a broken vase to explain my own trauma. The primary problem with how we view trauma and its damage is that we are not paying close enough attention to the cracks in the vase; there is too much emphasis put on *fixing* and not enough on understanding the root causes of human suffering. And, because most people involved in any form of psychological treatment are earning an income from it, there is a great deal of investment in being able to 'fix' trauma.

My father died on the floor in front of my crib when I was thirteen-months-old. I would not begin to examine this until I was in my late twenties. I worked full-time as a mental health counselor all through my 30's and 40's, and then began to also work on my own deep wounding. But it was not until three years ago that I attempted to make any contact with the military side of these issues. I had never talked to a World War II veteran about trauma, I had never met a survivor of the concentration camps, and was very far removed from the militarism and hero worship of war.

And then three years ago, on a summer night, for the first time I decided to immerse myself in the full reality of World War II. My conversations and experiences since then have only validated for me why I have such little interest in all that.

I have now attended the 50th reunion of the Ploesti mission, spoken with several veterans, met with a survivor of Auschwitz, met with a Jewish Rabbi, watched many films and documentaries about the war, received my father's World War II letters, and immersed myself just enough into militarism to know why I was keeping my distance.

Three years ago in July I had a phone conversation that left me very bewildered and angry. It was with one of the organizers of the annual reunion of the 94th bombardment group. I was late in contacting him but assumed he would welcome me speaking about my work in the field of PTSD, and commemorating my father with some sort of display. Instead he spoke to me in a way that implied he felt this has nothing to do with their reunion. Later, I would understand that he had no direct combat experience. He was flying the bombers after the war was over. He actually said that he considered the twenty-seven years that he was in service as 'having the best time of my life.'

This led me to the realization that denying combat trauma goes hand-in-hand with presenting a strong and constant military presence. When we watch a John Wayne movie we see him swaggering about, but not crying and having nightmares after a showdown in front of the saloon.

After the Ploesti reunion, I spoke with one of the veterans of the raid, and then with the son of one of my father's crew members who had recently died. In both conversations I was told those veterans had not suffered psychological trauma because of the war.

The surviving veteran I spoke with went down in the burning inferno of the oil refineries at Ploesti, essentially on fire. Because Romania was neutral, and because the bombs were not targeting civilians, they were treated well, with a visit from the Princess of Romania. He told me he had not suffered from his war wounds and thought himself to be the 'luckiest man on earth.' I asked him at what point he knew about the concentration camps. He did not have full-knowledge until after he was discharged. And then he really considered himself to be the luckiest man on earth compared to what they had gone through. I asked about the very real physical pain of being on fire. He said he had forgotten it long ago.

My father's wounds were almost entirely neuropsychiatric. He was not on fire, had no damage to his body other than fractured ribs. As I work to assimilate what the reality of returning home to Ohio and to a country celebrating victory and the end of the war meant to him, I know deep within myself that he felt he had no choice but to deny his trauma and to retreat very far into his own mind. There were plenty of John Waynes around. Norman was not one of them.

He spent ten years drinking himself into oblivion, and for the last year, I was the baby there in the crib watching him do it. And now, understanding his war trauma is one and the same as studying my own trauma from being his baby.

We need to look more directly at what psychological trauma is and quit trying to manipulate that reality to fit our own particular brand of fixing it. The path with this sort of healing is a labyrinth and finding our way within it has to become our own, and not someone else's. How trauma affects us is as infinitely complex as is the entire human condition.

Find your own way, and I will keep finding mine.

INTRODUCTION

Trauma; An emotional shock that creates
substantial and lasting damage to the
psychological development of the individual.
The American Heritage Dictionary

I have wanted to write a book about healing trauma for some time. I thought I would heal the traumas first, and then write the book. But as my understanding of trauma has deepened, I have come to see healing in a different way. I realize now that for me healing is something very different than what I once thought it might be. Lately, the image that comes to me is of a broken vase. If a vase repeatedly gets broken and then glued back together, it may still hold water, but it will never be whole again, not in the same way as an unbroken vase. I have had to work very hard for my own particular brand of wholeness, and, I am now whole.

Carl Jung wrote; "I would rather be whole than good." For most of my life, I was so far from whole that I didn't know what wholeness even meant. And now, I am whole. And, I am often still in pain. We are mistaken in believing that emotional pain is not real in the same way physical pain is. We can learn to use our pain in service to our own sanity.

Emotions are how we navigate life and relationships.

The photograph on the cover of this book is myself and my father, Christopher Norman Holweger, taken a few weeks before I watched him die. He was so very ill, suffering the physical and neuropsychiatric wounds from his service in World War II. He was too disabled to even take care of himself, and yet I was left alone with him every day. The last year of my father's life was the first year of my life. His woundedness was laid to rest with him. My woundedness is still with me.

Sometime on August 17th, 1942, my father left the family farm in Franklin, Ohio and went to the Army recruiting office in Cincinnati to enlist. He was twenty-two-years-old. Like countless men and women all over America, he was ready to step into the river that was the 2nd World War to do his share to stop fascism. He would return home to Franklin two years later. At the center of his brief military career was the bombing mission on the oil refineries of Ploesti, Romania. In fact, Ploesti was at the very center of my father's life. What happened to him aboard the plane called *Hadley's Harem* truly shattered his mind and soul so completely that he never recovered. It took another ten years for him to die of the wounds that were not seen, not physical, not treatable. He was a neuropsychiatric casualty of the Ploesti raid. The medical conditions which killed him were truly only a symptom of his shell-shock and depression. My father's death was never determined to be service-related. He was never properly memorialized. He is one of the forgotten soldiers of the war.

My father was three-quarters German, and, he went to war to stop the German Third Reich. Is that the way he saw it when he enlisted in 1942? We will never know. I assume it was much the same for him as it was for young men and women all over America. They were bored and restless and wanting to find a purpose bigger than they were. As one World War II veteran put it, by signing their name on the enlistment form they became men. By the end of the war, they had full knowledge of the extermination camps and all the rest of the horrors. By then, they knew exactly what they had fought for. On the 1940 census, when he was twenty, his occupation is "messenger boy, Western Union." He truly went from boy to man when he became a soldier.

At four o'clock on the morning of June 30th, 1955, my father awoke, struggling to breathe. My mother laid a quilt down on the floor, hoping it would be cooler there for him. Because we lived in a one-room apartment, my father laid down on that quilt right in front of my baby crib. I do not know exactly why there was blood. The death certificate says "probable coronary occlusion." He had been hospitalized several weeks before this and had his pancreas and part of his stomach removed, returning home to resume caring for me, with 56 stitches in his abdomen. But, he bled and struggled and then died. He was carried out in a body bag, and that was the end of my relationship with the only daddy I ever had. Understanding my father's suffering is a life-long process for me. It is only in understanding his wounds that I have been able to root out my own struggle with a lifetime of anxiety, depression, poor self-esteem... all the pathology that is so much a part of me. At the very center of my being is Ploesti. There are not words enough to make anyone understand this. Death took my daddy away and left me bereft in a world that thinks I don't remember.

After the raid on Ploesti, my father's plane crashed into the Mediterranean Sea. My father, his body bruised and battered, swam to the Turkish shore, helping to rescue the other wounded. Awaiting them on shore were fifteen "ragged Turkish peasants with ancient long rifles." During the days and nights that followed, before they were liberated by the British, the Turks kept them in a sort of tense and confused captivity. "All night long the wounded groaned when they were conscious. There was no medical aid. The camp fire burned them on one side, the wind froze them on the other." (1)

He was eventually sent back home to the states and several years later married my mother. I was born in 1954, their only child. They were very poor and he was too ill to work, so my mother worked long hours as a waitress to support us. We lived in a one-room apartment. I am not sure how it was that my family thought that my father, in the condition that he was in, was capable of being my primary caretaker, but they did. Times were hard and there were no social services.

Imagine that baby, for an entire year, witnessing everything that went on in that apartment; the grief and fear, the making love, the arguments. The mother leaving every morning filled with worry, the father drinking himself into oblivion, and the baby in the crib alone, not cared for, not held. As his own boundaries collapsed under the horror of mental breakdown and death, what was his relationship to his infant daughter?

A few years ago I went to see my father's sister in the nursing home in Ohio. I had not seen her since I was fifteen. My memory of her had been of a beautiful and strong Army nurse who had sent me gifts from her posts around the world. The woman I found in the home was frail, shrunken, and almost blind. Seeing her, I began to weep and could not stop, suddenly feeling the lifetime of denial my family had imposed upon me about my father.

I asked her to tell me about him. She sat there, not able to see me, but remembering her handsome brother who had gone off to war and returned wounded and broken. The image she painted for me was far more real than the idealized version of the war hero I had grown up with. Yes, he was a hero, but he was also alcoholic, and terribly sick with malaria and shell-shock (now called Post Traumatic Stress Disorder.) I now question this idea that he had malaria, believing it may have been my family's cover-up for his alcoholism.

As the tears streamed down my face, she told me all this. She said they would find him bailing water out of the bathtub saying "I'll save you buddy." I was the baby there in that room with him, either watching him have the flashbacks, or in the tub as he bailed the water out. My father's PTSD became mine. I asked her how they thought he could take care of me. She looked confused and said, "Well dear, your father had a lot of common sense."

I did not grow up knowing all that I just told you about my infancy. If you had met me thirty years ago and asked about my parents, I would have told you my mother lives in Kentucky and my father died when I was a baby. I would not have told you more because that is all I knew. You wouldn't have asked for more; no one ever did. I had no awareness that my infancy had anything to do with me. As a child, I became a mute. As a teenager, I ripped through life wanting to be dead.

I became a mother at the age of seventeen. As a young woman, I was so withdrawn into myself I was unknown to anyone, even me. There was a shroud placed over my being so that I would not know what I knew or remember seeing what I had seen.

If we are told we can't remember watching our father die in a pool of blood, then how will we remember anything else? This is where dissociation comes from, when we are not allowed to re-member; to bring back together the members, or parts, of who we are and what has made us.

I have become a private investigator into my own life, forcing my mother and aunts and uncles to give me back the pieces of my infancy that they still believe I have no right to because I was only a baby.

Had I grown up well, I could understand why they wouldn't want to help me dredge up the past.

But, I did not grow up well. I was very sickly as a little girl, and so very sad. At the age of twelve I became incorrigible; alcohol, drugs, a suicide attempt, promiscuity, a real adolescent hell. My depression has been life-long. Yet, my family, nor anyone else, was ever able to help me connect this with the original trauma.

Trauma often causes permanent damage to the organism; both physically and psychically. Some of the people in my life, when they hear me say this, believe I am only reinforcing the trauma, allowing myself to be victimized by it. What I have been victimized by is, first of all, the trauma itself, and secondly, the failure for others to understand. I have been twice-damned.

In my lifetime, I have seen all the ways that what we consider to be negative and dark gets denied and suppressed. This only compounds the damage. In a sense, the positive thinking movement, New Age spirituality, and the medical and pharmaceutical profession all are guilty of this. To feel pain, be depressed, have negative thoughts, be stuck in grief, to experience rage or moodiness, have anxiety . . . isn't alright and we must get rid of it as soon as possible. The failure with all these systems is that they only superficially address the problems.

When we are traumatized early through abuse, neglect, abandonment, the pain and terror that often occur during birth and womb-life, there is a very deep shame that develops where a healthy self should be. This is what John Bradshaw calls toxic shame. It is very complex and very real. When the world then continually tells us that there is something wrong with us for not being able to feel free and happy, it only reinforces this shame.

The other night I had a dream about a woman I know who is seriously engaged in meditation practice. Yes, she is blissfully serene and present. In the dream, I became so enraged with her I smashed something into her face. I awoke feeling just awful about it. How could I hit a meditator? Then I had to smile at myself. I guess all these years of living in northern California in the New Age mecca has finally gotten to me.

I suffer Post Traumatic Stress Disorder, from infancy. There has never been a time in my life when my experience hasn't been filtered through the original trauma. The vase was cracked from the beginning. I don't know that this can be understood by someone who has had a life without significant trauma, and who began life in wholeness and safety.

Our brains are created in the womb and in infancy. How we respond to subsequent stress is largely determined by our earliest environment.

This is from a book titled, *Inside the Brain;*

"Bad experiences effect the brain primarily through the stress hormones such as cortisol and adrenaline. Designed to respond to psychological or physical danger, these hormones prepare the body for fight or flight. Normally such changes are smooth: The brain and body are prepared for action when need be and then put back on an even keel when the danger is over. But when these hormones are overactive as a result of persistent stresses encountered during fetal development and early childhood, they can take over genetic regulation like a band of terrorists." (2)

Being exposed to stress does not make us more able to deal with it, it makes us less able. With each repeated trauma our internal integrity becomes increasingly compromised. We know that on some level. We hear stories of horrible catastrophes and understand that those victims will never be the same. Why then do we not see that there are traumas and wounds that others carry, from which they have been deeply damaged, that we cannot even begin to understand the full depth of that damage?

It was another tragedy that happened eighteen years ago that triggered the trauma of watching my father die. At that point, I had been in a marriage for several years, but we had separated. One night, I was in my apartment and my husband called, very distraught. He said there had been a shooting at his sister's house and he was on his way out there.

His sister and her husband were also going through a painful separation and weren't letting go of one another very well. She had been at her mother's for two weeks. She returned to try and talk things through one more time, and then decided to stay the night. When her husband left for work the next morning they agreed she should be gone when he got home. But instead, she stayed. He found her there, took out a gun and pointed it at her while he calmly explained that he was going to shoot her twice and then kill himself. And, that is what he did.

She was rushed by helicopter to the hospital. I was with her two days later holding her hand as her husband was cremated. I then went with my husband to clean up the mess left by the shootings. I wasn't prepared, still very much in shock myself. I knelt down with a bucket of water and a towel and cleaned up my brother-in-law's pool of blood from the floor.

And this was not my first brother-in-law who had died by shooting himself in the head. My sister Debby's husband in Kentucky had also committed suicide this way several years before. What she went through during that period has caused her irreparable damage.

During all of this that happened with my husband's sister, I remained convicted that I would follow through with my own divorce. My husband and I worked at the same psychiatric hospital. I had then been there for almost seven years, and because of an unfortunate set of circumstances, I had created enemies and didn't even know who they were because I no longer trusted anyone.

My brother-in-law's suicide happened in August. I had decided that I would resign my job in December, move back home to Kentucky, and file for the divorce. My relationships at work continued to deteriorate. I was not in therapy to deal with the horror of what I had experienced, and was not dealing with it, hardly even spoke to anyone about it. Then, two weeks before Christmas, my husband's other brother was electrocuted while working under a house.

At this point, I completely dissociated from the pain and reality of what was happening. But I functioned, quite well. My husband and I went to his mother's house. She was there with the wife and children of the brother who had just died. They were in shock. I became the dutiful daughter-in-law who knew what to do, but was completely cut off from my own feelings. I later was able to understand that I disconnected from the grief because I felt that I had no part in it, just like when my father died.

So all this had happened, an attempted murder, a suicide, divorcing my husband, being ostracized at work, another brother-in-law being electrocuted, all within four months. Inwardly, I had left the scene of the accident. On the outside, I probably seemed "just fine."

I remember being at Macy's and shopping for the perfect pair of black heels to wear to both the funeral and to the staff Christmas party where I would be saying goodbye to people who I wanted to spit at. I then took the Greyhound bus back to Kentucky, rented a farm, continued to work in psychiatric treatment, and had a few affairs. Deep inside there was my voice, the voice of the infant girl I had been, screaming at me,

"Stop. I need you to stop and listen to me."

On the day I had the breakdown, I had driven sixty miles from work in a beat-up old Nova. My back was in agony. I had lost so much weight that I had gone from my normal one-hundred-twenty pounds down to about ninety. I was broke and broken. There I was, for the first time in my adult life living right in the middle of my family, and I had a breakdown without ever asking them for help or telling them about what had happened in California.

Dissociation can take many different forms. The most extreme is when the mind actually begins splitting into different personalities, what was formerly called Multiple Personality Disorder. It is only the most extreme forms of traumatic experience that cause the mind to mobilize in such a way as to create separate personalities. But, somewhere just this side of splitting off into other personalities are states that more closely resemble amnesia. The body is still able to function; to function very well in fact. We can go through the motions and no one ever realizes that there isn't anyone there. Memory isn't being recorded or retrieved in the same way. Who we are as an organism continues to live and breathe, but our emotional self has scattered to the far regions of the mind. This is how I describe being in a "fugue" state.

There have been a few times in my life that I entered into some sort of dissociative state bordering on fugue. After the incidents happened in California and I moved back home to live in the woods, I was in such a state. It isn't that I have no memories. Some of my memories from that time are very real. But, I was so split off while I was going through those experiences that I wasn't in my body or in my emotions. I was headed for a breakdown.

One night I was in my bedroom and sound asleep when I was awakened by the sound of someone whistling for the old farm dogs that slept outside. I awoke, looked at the clock and saw that it was four o'clock in the morning, then heard a car motor running outside. I immediately knew that some of the local drunks had come to harass me, and probably worse. Someone started knocking loud on the front door. I went into the bathroom where I could look out on to the front porch. I looked through the slats of the blinds and saw that it was a couple of the local addict-drunks who I was sure were there to rape me. In that instant, my anxiety shot so high that I had my first real panic attack.

I think it is curious that I was looking through those slats, just as I had been looking through the slats of my crib as my father died. They eventually left and I called the deputy sheriff.

After the breakdown (which I now call the breakthrough) I promised myself I would never again ask for anyone's permission to own the experience, in whatever form it takes, of my father's illness and death.

It was during that breakdown year that I finally let the terror and grief about my father come to the surface. Because of what I had gone through with my brother-in-law's suicide, I was finally able to connect with my first trauma. It was the pool of blood of one man that connected me with the pool of blood of the other.

The way I see it is that we are each of us a fragile archeological site holding the memories of our lives. Our minds need to be examined only with the greatest of care. If we allow in what is unskillful, impatient, heavy-handed, the site will be contaminated. This is what happens to far too many people who in their quest to heal have let in so many helpers that the original ground has become muddy with all the helping. On the other hand, it is important to honor what comes up in ourselves, and to recognize it as some answer that is trying to be born, or some past wound that is asking for healing.

In her book, *If Someone Speaks, It Gets Lighter,* Lynda Share writes;

"That the present is determined by the past (psychic determinism) is a concept at the very foundation of psychoanalysis. It implies that the past is somehow registered and stored in the mental (or somatic) apparatus. But how far "past" does "past" go? Does it go to the very beginning of life? When, in fact, does human mental life begin, and how early is a "memory" of that life possible? We do not have definitive answers to these questions, but we now have a compilation of both research data and psychoanalytic writings suggesting that "mental life" begins much earlier than we ever imagined." (3)

Several years ago I attended a congress on Prenatal and Perinatal Psychology and Health. I helped set up the bookstore for the conference. There were hundreds of titles to sort and put on the shelves, all pertaining to pregnancy, birth, and early development. We decided to arrange them in a timeline around the room, beginning on the left with conception and then continuing through birth and neonatal development. I became very familiar with the titles so that I could direct others to what they were looking for. Many times I walked back and forth around the room. Each time that I walked "backward" so to speak, from infancy, to birth, to conception, I became increasingly aware that who we are doesn't even really start with conception.

What is the "beyond?" Where was our soul before it entered our mother's womb? What is the "ancestral imprint?"

I have now read many volumes of literature about early development and trauma. By doing so, I slowly, and painfully, have pieced myself together. The symptoms and behaviors I have had with me for a lifetime now make sense in the context of the extremely traumatizing bonding that I experienced with my father.

Am I saying that we can't heal? No. What I'm saying is that our healing might look like something very different than what we thought it might, or what others think it should. Healing begins when we shift into self-acceptance, stop denying the truth about who we are, and quit giving others the power to define our sense of ourselves.

I am a *"hard work miracle."* This is the title of Stephen Johnson's book, which I will be citing later; *Characterological Transformation; The Hard Work Miracle.* (4)

My healing has taken profound, deep, and extensive work, psychologically and spiritually. It is work I have done almost entirely alone, within the depths of my being, my primary support being the written literature left to us by almost two-hundred years of psychology and neurobiology research.

This book is a testament to my traumas, and to my healing, such as it is. Also, it is the chronicle of my career over the last thirty years as a counselor. I have chosen to work with those who have been most damaged. People who are extremely wounded very often end up in "the system." They become institutionalized in psychiatric hospitals, drug treatment programs, and prisons. And, these are the places I have carried out my role as counselor, educator, and minister.

I am deeply grateful to the scholars, researchers, and teachers who have helped me find my way back to myself. When the rest of the world was saying "Forget what happened when you were little; get on with your life," they were saying, "Keep digging, you will find yourself." I owe them my life.

John Bowlby, Alice Miller, Sigmund Freud, Carl Jung, Candace Pert, Richard Restak, Peter Nathanielsz, John Bradshaw, Lynda Share, Lenore Terr, Thomas Verny, Peter Levine, Margaret Mahler, Stephen Johnson, Allan Schore, D. W. Winnicott Elizabeth Loftus, Judith Lewis Herman, James Masterson (to mention only a few) . . .

Thank you for giving me the tools for digging my way out.

CHAPTER ONE
Memory
Letting Go of Letting Go

There seems to be a wide-spread belief in the necessity of letting go of the past in order to achieve inner peace. This belief is very frustrating to me. We cannot, and should not even want to, let go of our earliest experience. It is the template on which we were made. People who have suffered extreme brain damage that has destroyed memory systems, they have let go of the past. I can't imagine that being a desirable state. We are, in a very real sense, our memories.

If by letting go what is meant is that we are no longer tormented by the past, do not let it define who we are becoming, then I agree that this would be helpful. For me the problem is in the fine line drawn between not being tormented, and being in complete denial, which is the state that was forced upon me about my infancy. I once heard it said that we are all suffering under a post-hypnotic trance induced at infancy.

This brings us to the central mystery of how we can heal that which we don't consciously remember. Sigmund Freud wrote in *The Psychopathology of Everyday Life;*

"In my opinion we take the fact of infantile amnesia, the loss, that is of the memories of the first years of our life, much too easily; and we fail to look upon it as a strange riddle." (5)

For me, this riddle is no longer theoretical, but the way out of the maze of a lifetime of emotional pain created by the traumatic circumstances of my early life. If I were able to look back from the vantage point I am at now and see that I left behind me an untroubled and successful life, then maybe I would be able to let go of the past. But when I look back at my life, I know that I have to continue to understand how my decisions, my relationships with others, and my sense of self were all directly influenced by my infancy; the time that I can't remember.

Many contemporary researchers delineate between "explicit" and "implicit" memory. Explicit, or declarative, memories, are those that can consciously be recalled. Implicit memories are those memories that are not so readily available to conscious recall. They are subconscious. Therefore, all very early memories are implicit.

The difference between the two memory systems is this; if you are asked to remember your first day of school, you might be able to recall that your teacher wore a blue dress, smelled like roses, and that you cried and felt lonely when your mother left.

However, if you can't recall the conscious "explicit" memory you might say you remember nothing about it. But suppose sometimes when you see the color blue or smell a rose you feel inexplicably lonely. This is implicit memory.

Memory and learning are much the same. To "learn" something means to encode it somehow so that it can be used for future reference. Learning is memorizing the alphabet so we can say each letter by name. But, it also means that if as a child every time you cried you got hit, then you "learned" not to cry. Or, if as a child you touched something hot and got burned, your hand "learned" to pull away from hot things. It holds the memory.

Dreams are one of the ways that we can work with our healing, both by working to understand what the dream is showing us about ourselves, and by changing our dream state through a process called lucid dreaming.

The first time I experienced lucid dreaming was many years ago. I was having recurrent dreams of being raped. One night before I went to sleep I gave myself a very simple suggestion. I knew that on some level I had control of what happened in the dream. I suggested to myself that the next time I dreamt of being raped I would take control. That very night I dreamt I was being chased by a rapist. I turned and confronted him and he ran away. A few weeks later I had another rape dream and this time I disappeared down a "manhole" (the kind that is in the middle of a street.) I have never had a rape dream since then. (Talk about symbolism...a manhole!)

For many years I dreamt of abandoned babies. They came to me over and over. Sometimes, in the dream, a stranger would give me a baby to protect. In other dreams, I would see a baby being hurt and remove it from harm. In some dreams the babies were my own two children.

Once, the dream baby was repulsive, only a few inches long, with a huge head and tiny deformed limbs. It was dying. Sometime after that I was looking through a book on childhood development and found a picture just like my dream baby. It was a fourteen week-old fetus. From deep inside myself I knew that it meant I needed to go back to where the damage had started.

Does that mean that I have to somehow "remember" it? I don't think so. What it does mean is that I have to own all of myself, even the self in my mother's womb. That is the root.

There is no one else that can ever be inside our own heads but us. I am the storehouse for my emotional and somatic experience. The woman I am today remembers and is influenced by who I've been for the past year. And the woman I was a year ago remembered the previous year, all the way back through my life, each self remembering an earlier self.

When I look back at my early childhood now, of course the memories are blurred and disjointed. But, who I was at five remembered who I was at three, and who I was at three still remembered my father. Now, instead of saying *I remember my father,* I say, *I have memory of my father.* Not the plural, memories. But memory. When I became old enough to formulate abstract questions, at about age three, I asked my mother and aunt, "Why did my daddy die?"

I remember the very clear feeling that I was not supposed to ask that and knowing that they didn't have an answer. I asked because my father was still very much a part of my experience. I remember struggling inside my toddler brain to make the words come out.

At about the same time, I was having a recurrent dream/memory (I don't know which) of him watching over me. I was lying in bed and he was a few feet away, in the living room. He sat on a footstool covered with purple fabric. He wore a white shirt and grey slacks. He was very emaciated. His face was sad, his hair line receding as it had been at the end of his life.

The subject of memory has eluded, baffled, and occupied, philosophers, psychologists, and neurologists for centuries. They have designed and conducted experiments, compiled statistics, drawn up schema, developed and refuted theories, all in an effort to understand memory.

How is experience stored and retrieved? Where exactly is it stored? What is the mechanism whereby some information is stored but easily called to consciousness if needed, some is repressed, and some seemingly forgotten? How does the sorting out process happen? What is it that does the sorting?

There are memories from my childhood, not just about my father, that remain a mystery to me. One that always comes to mind when I think about memory is this. When I was little, we would sometimes cross through the woods behind my grandparent's house in Kentucky, and up a hill to visit a relative we called Aunt Becky. As I was growing up, I distinctly remembered that on several occasions we had gone beyond Aunt Becky's, through the woods, and come upon a little shack overlooking the creek. Each time, there had been an old couple sitting there on the porch in rocking chairs. I did see them. The memory was real.

I left Kentucky at nineteen and was very removed for many years. Sometimes I would wonder about that old couple and their shack, but it wasn't until I was in my thirties that I asked my uncle about them. He told me that there wasn't anyone over there like that. I couldn't get them out of my mind, and the following year asked my aunt, the oldest of my mother's siblings. I described in detail how we walked to get there, and what the shack and the couple looked like. She looked amazed and told me that, yes, they had been there just like that.

It was my great-great-grandfather, John Johnson, and his second wife, Rosa. But, they had died long before I was even born and the shack had long since been fallen down. Was I having an "ancestral memory?" Did all the ghosts I lived with as a child fill me with their memories?

It is because of these kinds of experiences, memories that can't be accounted for by even normal explanations of memory, that I have become fascinated by the study of memory, in particular, my own. I'm not sure that we can limit our ideas about the storage of memory to only what happens in the individual brain. There is a collective memory; there is God's memory. In that sense, it may be that our entire history as humans is recorded on some sort of template. That would explain archetypes.

There was another experience that happened six years ago that convinced me that I can't even begin to fathom how my father is recorded in my mind. At the time, I was doing intense work through dreams and meditation to try and bring up memories of him. I was living on a farm in Kentucky, and on that day I was sitting alone in the orchard doing a breathing exercise my daughter had taught me.

The purpose of the exercise is to release emotional energy. The exercise is to forcibly expel all the air from your lungs and then to go as long as possible without taking another breath. After doing this for several moments, my chest started hurting. (My mother says that when my father died he kept complaining of not being able to get a breath.)

I had my eyes closed. I could see energy sort of swirling around in my head, and then suddenly, an image of my father was before me in my mind's eye. He was standing there, white shirt, gray flannel pants, like photographs I have of him. I knew, and knew absolutely, that at that moment I was experiencing what my father had felt as he was dying.

I was living with a man named Jerry at that time. The image came of my father, and then was instantly replaced by an image of Jerry. It went back and forth like that several times, my father, then Jerry, then my father. For the rest of my life I will wonder what would have happened had I stayed with it. But, I panicked and opened my eyes.

"In broad outline, there are basically two kinds of views about the neural basis for the retention of experience or learning. One view supposes that an experience sets up a continuing electrical activity in appropriate neural circuits and that the persistence of these active circuits is coordinate with the persistence of our memory of the experience coded in this way. When this active trace process stops, we lose that memory. We may call this the "dynamic" view of the engram, or long-term memory trace. Opposed to it is the "structural" view, that learning consists in some enduring physical, structural, or biochemical change in the nervous system, and that this physical change will persist even when the original neuronal circuits responsible for its having been established in the first place have returned to relative quiescence following the initial experience." (6)

These kinds of technical formulations about learning and memory are fascinating, but there is a deeper, more far-reaching element that gets left out of the discussion. Information gets stored, repressed, or forgotten. What makes the choice?

In his book, *The Invention of Memory* (which I quoted from above) Israel Rosenfield opens by addressing this issue, citing the importance of Freud's views about the impact of emotion on memory;

"The full significance of this discovery may have been missed by contemporary neuroscientists and psychologists. For Freud was in effect describing the functioning of the limbic system (a set of interconnected structures deep inside the brain), long before discoveries in the 1930's suggested its importance in emotional behavior. More recently, limbic structures have been found to effect memory as well." (7)

Of course, the whole theory of repressed memory is now suspect because of the contamination that has happened as the result of overly zealous therapists helping to create false memories in clients, particularly around the issue of incest. But, when a pendulum swings to an extreme in one direction, it has to then swing back to the other extreme. For so long there was an extreme denial about the extent and prevalence of child abuse. Now, we have gone too far in the other direction.

Elizabeth Loftus, a research psychologist who is considered an expert in the field of memory, thoroughly examines this controversy in *The Myth of Repressed Memory*;

"Something has gone wrong with therapy, and because that something has to do with memory, I find myself at the center of an increasingly and fractious controversy. On the one side are the "True Believers," who insist that the mind is capable of repressing memories and who accept without reservation or question the authenticity of recovered memories. On the other side are the "Skeptics," who argue that the notion of repression is purely hypothetical and essentially untestable, based as it is on unsubstantiated speculation and

anecdotes that are impossible to confirm or deny."
(8)

Just as I had finished reading her book and was pondering the question of repressed memory, I got a call from a friend of mine. As we were chatting about times past we got on to the subject of a night we had gone out with another friend several years before; three women friends out for an evening of dancing and fun.

We had ended up at a bar where a bride-to-be was having her drunken and debauched bachelorette party. The entire bar joined in the fun. I have told the story about that night at least a dozen times. As I was talking to my friend, she asked, "Do you remember why we went out that night?" I drew a complete blank, there was absolutely no information available to me. She then reminded me of the circumstances leading up to our night out. I had planned a party at my house and no one came except these two women friends. My party had been boycotted because I had left my husband, and out of loyalty to him, our mutual friends were upset with me and didn't come.

The experience had been so painful and humiliating that I had totally repressed it. Suddenly, it all came back, even the hors d' oeuvres I had laid out on the table. This conversation and the memories it unleashed seemed significant to me because it verified the power of the mechanism of repression. But, it was also significant because once again I was reminded of how the universal mind of God has it all recorded and assisted me in that moment to know the truth about repression. My friend was the angel delivering the message.

This is why, when it comes right down to it, the only real evidence we have for anything is in our own being and if we are going to understand the human mind it is important to always filter knowledge through our own experience. Some scientists disparagingly refer to this as anecdotal; just a story that someone is telling that can't be substantiated. It could be that one of the reasons they so quickly brush aside the knowledge others have come to through their own experiences is that they haven't had similar experiences themselves.

If you haven't experienced telepathy, for instance, how could you believe it in someone else? If you haven't witnessed your own mind repressing a memory, then you would be less willing to believe it in others. If you are not soul-full, how can you recognize the soul of another?

In *Waking the Tiger*, Peter Levine writes;

"Buffeting between the extreme polarities of heaven and hell generates the rhythm essential for the transformation of trauma." (9)

In my experience, the "hell" is going back down into the pain, shame, and terror of the past, wrestling with it just like Jacob in the Old Testament wrestled with the angel. "Heaven" is when I am able to come fully into the present moment to experience freedom and joy. (This is not Levine's explanation of heaven and hell, but my own.)

As we find ways to gently swing back and forth between these two polarities we generate a healing energy that may be the closest to being healed that trauma sufferers can feel. Instead of this, I think many people stay stuck somewhere in between; not willing to fully experience past hurts, but not able either to experience the liberation of the present moment.

Levine writes about the physiological mechanisms of trauma. When we are threatened, just like any other animal, we have three choices; to flee, to fight, or to freeze (become immobile.) His approach is very cautious. This is why I've been so drawn to his work. Regression therapies that encourage going back fully into memories, as with combat veterans who have flashbacks, can cause more trauma.

Physiologically, our mind/body can be re-traumatized, believing that the experience is actually happening all over again. What all the research seems to be uncovering is that affectively influenced memory (memories with an intense emotional component) activate a different system and are stored differently, and perhaps even have a different retrieval system due to some mechanism we might call repression.

There are many modalities being practiced for the treatment of trauma, and many practitioners. There is some elaborate experimentation going on in our global search to heal mental pain. Ultimately, it is an inside job. No matter what we take in from outside ourselves, the change has to occur in our own mind and body and heart.

Experimentation may seem like a harsh word to use in this context. It isn't. Experiment simply means to try something without knowing what the outcome will be. The entire history of psychological treatment has been one long experiment beginning sometime in the eighteenth century. Early practitioners used means that seem very offensive to us now; bloodletting, frontal lobe lobotomies, hot mustard plasters, male doctors putting "hysterical" female patients on display. The kinds of techniques we are now exploring for the treatment of trauma; rebirthing, Rapid Eye Movement, Neural Linguistic Programming; may seem just as strange one hundred years from now. Only time will tell what is helping.

The real question then is how do we go back to work with trauma in all the ways it is stored in our mind and body? Sometimes, people who have suffered extreme trauma, seem to then snap right out of it, as though it never happened. This is how people who are in shock behave. Think of a woman who has just been told her husband has been killed, and then she gets up with a smile on her face and asks if anyone wants a cup of tea. Her system is so overloaded and shocked that she has dissociated from the knowledge.

Healing isn't about letting go, but it is about letting be. Our past will always continue to be there. We can't make it not so. We can't make our past not have happened, but we can transform it.

I once worked with another counselor who had tattoos covering about 75% of her body. She had a very pain-filled childhood and was addicted and out of control by the time she reached adolescence. She eventually ended up in prison. By the time she was incarcerated, she had tattoos all over her body which revealed her attitude; knives and skulls and other images of darkness. While in prison, she made a commitment to her own recovery. Realizing it would be difficult and costly to remove the tattoos, she decided to transform them. Once she was free again, she had her body art transformed into flowers and butterflies and oriental goddesses.

I think that is what real healing looks like. We don't make our past traumas, wounds, and experiences disappear. But we can accept them with all their intricacies, patterns, and entanglements, like a complex spider web woven through our lives and soul. By owning our past, we then are free to be creative and resourceful in how we transform it.

There is another aspect to why we can't let go of the past; because others hold memories of us as well as we do. I may be ready to let go of, for instance, the arrogant self I used to be, but there are people in my life who still hold that experience of me. I'm not sure that the amends making that we use in 12-step meetings is quite as simple as I once thought. Other's experiences of us and with us get woven into the complex fabric of their beings as well. Just as what we might have done to hurt them took place over time, our amending it might also need time. It can't be forced.

This is most apparent to me in my relationship to my children. They did not have perfect childhoods, and suffered their own traumas, partly as the result of having me for a mother. For many years now they have been processing the history we shared together when they were growing up. As their memories surface to consciousness, they have needed me to be available to work through with them their pain and anger. I have no control over what comes up or how they do the work of their childhoods.

It has been disheartening to me to see that sometimes other parents of adult children aren't able to be available to do this work. Even though they themselves might be in recovery or therapy to deal with childhood issues, they fail to see that they have some responsibility to go back into the pain that happened in the past that their children are now beginning to deal with.

We don't have to let go. For me there has been a liberation in just knowing that for myself. By going back down inside myself to unbury the memories of my father, I have found more of myself.

When trauma happens, the soul doesn't leave, it splinters. It becomes so hidden within the labyrinth of our own being that there is only one way to find it. It requires going back down inside to our innermost being to seek out the dark, forbidden places; down into a dungeon where the stones have grown over with moss.

It can be scary. I do not know of any other way. As we do this memory work, it is for us to decide who we will let in to help, who we will expose ourselves to. Trying to do it all alone can be risky. But so can trusting other people to guide us on our healing journey. Like everything else, it is a question of balance.

The best we can do is to educate ourselves about healing and therapeutic modalities, move cautiously, trust our own instincts, and when the demons come in the middle of the night, face them with as much courage as we can.

During my own healing process, I have become drawn to the work of Alice Miller. Miller was born in Poland to a Jewish family, and escaped the holocaust by living under an assumed name in Warsaw. She trained in traditional psychoanalysis, and worked as a psychoanalyst for twenty years. She began denouncing the psychoanalytic movement of the time, coming out strongly in her assertion that it blamed the child and idealized the parents. In *Banished Knowledge: Facing Childhood Injuries,* she explained that it was the spontaneous painting she took up in 1973 that "gave me the first unadulterated access to my early reality. In my paintings I came face to face with the terrorism exerted by my mother, at the mercy of which I had lived for so many years." (10)

I must interject here that she was reacting to the practice as it had developed originally by Freud and others. In theory, psychoanalysis is all about uncovering infant and childhood trauma, coming out of repression, and examining unconscious content. In my own healing work, I have not been in formal psychoanalysis, but have been my own Jungian analyst, drawing on the work of one of my heroes, Carl Jung.

Miller focused much of her work and research on the cruel and repressive childrearing practices in

Germany that fed young people into the war machine.

She quotes Adolf Hitler;

"My pedagogy is hard. What is weak must be hammered away. In my fortresses of the Teutonic Order a young generation will grow up before which the world will tremble. I want the young to be violent, domineering, undismayed, cruel. The young must be all these things. They must be able to bear pain. There must be nothing weak or gentle about them. The free, splendid beast of prey must once again flash from their eyes. I want my young people strong and beautiful. That way I can create something new." (11)

My initial interest in Miller's theories had everything to do with my father's shell-shock due to World War II, and the fact that three of his grandparents were born in Germany. Her concept of an "enlightened witness" resonated with me in that I had no such witness in my childhood. By emerging as a trauma educator and writer, I am asking my readers to be that witness, as she did also. In *Drama of the Gifted Child*, she wrote;

"Experience has taught us that we have only one enduring weapon in our struggle against mental illness; the emotional discovery and emotional acceptance of the truth in the individual and unique history of our childhood." (12)

She writes extensively about Hitler in *For Your Own Good;*

"But we must go one step further if we are to understand the origins of a lifelong insatiable hatred such as consumed Adolf Hitler. We must leave the familiar territory of drive theory and address the question of what takes place in a child who is humiliated and demeaned by his parents on the one hand and on the other is commanded to respect and love those who treat him in this fashion and under no circumstances to give expression to his suffering. Although something so absurd would scarcely be expected of an adult (except in pronouncedly sado-masochistic relationships,) this is exactly what parents expect of their children in most cases, and in previous generations they were rarely disappointed. In the earliest stage of life, it is possible for a child to forget about the extreme acts of cruelty he or she has endured and to idealize their perpetrator. But the nature of the subsequent enactment reveals that the whole history of early persecution was stored up somewhere; the drama now unfolds in front of the spectators with an amazing resemblance to the original situation but under another guise: in the reenactment, the child who was once persecuted now becomes the persecutor." (13)

Alice Miller died in 2010. Now, her son Martin, has written his own book, *The True 'Drama of the Gifted Child'; the Tragedy of Alice Miller.* It seems to me that he has remarkable insight in separating her inadequacies as a mother from who she was as a theorist and an activist for the rights of children.

Alice Miller suffered her own traumas because of the persecution of Jews, and suppressed her anger towards her own mother from a need to protect their family from their real enemies. She underwent psychoanalysis and then became a theorist in an effort to explain how her childhood had damaged her, and then to further our understanding of these complex issues. And, her own ability to be a nurturing and supportive mother may have been diminished because of her early trauma. Mine certainly was.

This really elucidates one of the schisms in psychology. We believe that because someone understands their own trauma they then are exempt from acting that trauma out, especially with those of us who are trauma educators. It may seem at first glance that Alice Miller was a hypocrite. Instead, her son's book needs to be studied as further evidence of the persistence of trauma over a lifetime, as apparently was the case with his mother.

Several months ago I arranged a meeting with a ninety-four-year-old woman who is a survivor of Auschwitz. She is the first survivor I have ever met. As we sat on her patio having coffee and some fruit, watching butterflies in the blossoming trees, she described the horrors of being taken into Auschwitz when she was seventeen. Her father was beaten and killed in front of her. Her mother and several siblings died there. I asked to see her serial number. She rolled up her sleeve and there it was, branded on her arm. In that instant, it all finally seemed to be real to me. Not that I ever questioned the reality of the holocaust. But my father's suffering and wartime experience had always seemed so surreal. It was by looking at her branded arm that it became real for me.

I had so hoped that she would understand the nature of my need to meet her, and have some understanding of the depth of the trauma I suffered as the infant daughter of a Ploesti survivor. But I really don't think she did.

This presents another schism in trauma study. It is almost impossible to not rate the level of traumas; whose trauma was worse? The holocaust that happened to Jewish people (and others) in World War II was so horrific that all other trauma seems to pale by comparison. What African slaves and Indians suffered right here in America was also a holocaust.

My work to uncover and heal infant trauma is understood by almost no one. I am always swimming upstream against one false attitude after another. The idea that because infancy isn't "remembered" it therefore can't hurt us goes against every bit of reality. It many ways infant trauma does more damage precisely because the memories can't be consciously accessed.

In a world that seems to believe that peace comes from letting go of our own personal past, it's difficult to explain that my peace comes from fighting every day of my life to reclaim memories that are buried deep in the recesses of my being.

Much of my work is sort of reconstructive. By claiming as much as I can of the facts of my early life, I then can connect that with my very real feeling states. When the two match up, there is enormous relief for me.

For instance, I was kept in a crib and suffered some moderate to extreme neglect. My father became morbidly ill at the time my normal development would have had me out of the crib and exploring the world of that apartment, or the yard or park. But he was too ill to give me that freedom. Knowing this, my lifelong pattern of not being able to tolerate confinement or being held down in one place too long makes complete sense.

At thirteen-months-old, I would have been entering into the phase called *rapprochement* as identified in object-relations theory. Picture a normal toddler. She ventures away from her father to explore the next room, looking back to make sure he is still there. Her secure attachment to him allows her to explore, knowing he will be there when she toddles or crawls back.

This phase, in normal and healthy development, is when the child overcomes ambivalence regarding the need for autonomy versus the security of having the primary figure (mother or father) always right there.

The incredible gains made by an interdisciplinary approach to the study of the infant and young child now makes it possible to, not only look at outward behaviors, but to chart these phases in the very cells and molecules of what it taking place in the infant brain.

What happened in my infant brain as I watched my father die and be carried away forever? Before, he was there, always there. But then there was the time he was hospitalized. Then he returned, still there in the apartment, always in the room with me. Very ill, probably in a drunken stupor much of the time, having flashbacks, but very much there.

When I look at the photograph on the cover of this book, my heart breaks all over again for that baby. I try my best to remember being held in his weak and unsteady arms, or holding his frail hand. When I witnessed his death, I went hurtling into an abyss, and I still am.

It is as if my father is just on the other side of a partially opened door, waiting for me to find him. I can almost see him, and I always can feel his presence there, waiting, sad, broken. With each phase of my healing journey, the door opens just a little more. He becomes more real, not less. My infant self wants to reclaim her father. And, I am the only one who can open that door for her.

CHAPTER TWO
Grief
You Can't Break a Broken Heart

There is a photograph of myself, taken a few months after I watched my father die. The photographer has me sitting on a step, my little arm placed in an artificial pose. There is so much pain and confusion in that baby's face, her expression says, *I don't know what's going on in this world but maybe if I'm real quiet and do what they say no one else will die and leave me.*

I developed a secret inner life where no one could find me, where I would be safe. So often, I felt more intelligent than others but knew I wasn't supposed to let anyone know that. This private self took form and grew, separating me from others. She was brilliant, sad, and very alone.

I was suffering with childhood depression but no one could see it. I was not allowed to express feelings of sadness. Instead, it manifested in physical illness, withdrawal, and aversion to school. I missed 60 days of school in the 1st grade. I remember being sent to my room for crying and being told to "not have such a long face."

And I'm not talking about crying because I couldn't have a piece of candy or go out to play. I mean sadness just coming over me as a little girl and needing to cry and be held. It was driven so deep in me that I no longer just felt sad; I was the sadness.

The causes for my depression were multiple. During my prenatal and infant development, my parents were very stressed. They could not give me a sense of security because they did not have it to give.

"Stress, for instance, through its hormonal inter-mediaries, turns on genes that leave a memory trace of a bad feeling. Then along comes a lesser stress that triggers the same memory trace and reinforces it. Now, instead of a lousy feeling, the person gets depressed. Finally, after repeated reinforcements, the memory trace takes on a life of its own, firing willy-nilly and producing depression without any outside trigger." (14)

There is no time in our lives that we are more dependent and helpless than while we are in the womb, and during our earliest development. The way we are cared for then, the condition of our mother's environment and then the larger environment, will largely determine how we will respond to the world for the remainder of our lives.

A newborn baby is a complex bundle of tissue sorting itself out at an incredibly fast speed. It is estimated that 250,000 brain cells (neurons) are being created every minute during certain periods of fetal development.

That bundle of tissue encapsulates a soul; a soul that I believe experiences and perhaps even records all that happens to it, or around it, in ways that with our limited understanding we may never know. So we are born into a body that is entirely dependent upon others to sustain its every need. That newborn is powerless to obtain food, remove itself from danger, provide for itself the sensory stimulation that is crucial for healthy development. It cannot recognize language or name anything so it is lost in a sea of voices. Its emotional and psychological state is mostly determined by the state of its caretakers.

In her book, *Trauma and Recovery*, Judith Herman identifies three stages of healing;

"Recovery unfolds in three stages. The central task of the first stage is the establishment of safety. The central task of the second stage is remembrance and mourning. The central task of the third stage is reconnection with ordinary life." (15)

I have become very aware of these stages in my own life as recurrent traumas have happened. But this brings me back to the point I made in the introduction. With each successive traumatic experience, we become increasingly compromised in our ability to "heal" because deep inside ourselves we increasingly see the world as being unsafe. These stages are not very often as well-defined as we might like them to be.

Shortly after I began to do the healing work connected with my infancy, I experienced the other set of traumas. I then tried to rely on my life-long coping mechanism which was to find sanctuary in the forest. As I mentioned in the introduction, I fled from the traumas that happened in California and rented a house deep in the woods of Kentucky.

After the breakdown I returned to California again for several months. The panic attacks were so bad that I suffered insomnia for a month-and-a-half, couldn't eat, cried constantly, and simply did not want to live anymore. I eventually came to see the anxiety that I experienced during that time as the energy that had been suppressed and which was needed to push up through the mass of denial put upon me regarding my father's illness and death.

I then tried once more to seclude myself in the forest. I returned to Kentucky where I lived for a year in an army tent in the woods. The land I lived on was owned by two brothers. Their presence kept me safe and allowed me to go through what I needed to. I felt like I was going insane. But, I faced it. I thought if I am going insane, then I will let it happen right here, I'm not running anymore. What the "insanity" felt like was such incredibly intense emotional pain that I thought my mind was going to splinter from it.

Confronting that pain was what I had to go through to get to the other side. I have never felt since then that I am insane. Yes, I am in pain, but I am not insane.

The environment I was born into, a one-room apartment with a mother and father living with the constant stress of poverty and my father's illness, alcoholism, and eventual death, was not safe. I have felt a profound sense of not being safe my entire life. It is not safe for a one-year-old infant to experience the reality of death of the being she was most bonded with. There is a sort of terror at the center of my being that I can't ever really describe. Biologically speaking, the structure in my brain called the amygdala was activated too early.

I have two younger sisters, each of us spaced six years apart. Our mother did not marry either of their fathers, so we all three grew up without our natural fathers. Our youngest sister was given up for adoption, and then reunited with us just a few years ago. We each suffered in our childhoods and we have each struggled with different sets of problems.

Our mother worked long, hard hours to support us. She waitressed, sometimes six and seven days a week, and then took in ironing on the side. I think that she felt that as long as she was working she wouldn't fall apart. There was so little help for bereaved widows. My father died and some part of her died with him.

Our larger extended family was outwardly very close and happy, but there wasn't much emotional expression allowed. I can't ever remember as a child seeing a grown up hurt or talk abusively to any of us, (I have thirty-seven cousins on my mother's side.) But, I also can't remember seeing any real displays of emotion. I was an emotional orphan.

My mother herself was a traumatized infant, born prematurely in 1930 to a poor family in the hills of Kentucky. She was delivered at home in the middle of winter in sub-zero temperature and weighed a little more than two pounds. I once asked a physician what a two-pound baby would look like. He held out his hand and said,

"Something between a fetus and a baby."

Her mother, my grandmother, was not a nurturing woman. My mother's bonding was severely damaged. It is hard to give your own infants what you never had.

The circumstances surrounding my father's death were the unfortunate outcome of World War II. He was a war hero who died a tragic death. My parents were doing the best they could. But, I also know that if somehow the adults had included me in the grief process, had allowed my questions as I was growing up, had simply recognized how deeply I had been affected, then the trauma would not have been compounded the way it has been. I would have grown up having more tools and resources available for trying to ascertain what reality is. I witnessed my father's dead body being taken out of the room in a body bag and then my family sealed up my feelings the same as they sealed his coffin.

When I was twelve, there were three events in my life that propelled me from the mute and docile child I had been into an incorrigible and suicidal teenager. My mother became pregnant and was not married (for the 2nd time) my grandfather died, and I was molested by a nineteen-year-old heroin addict.

I began drinking, and then by the age of fourteen turned to drugs. I really had no concern for what I took, only that it make me feel anything other than the pain I had carried inside.

It's difficult to concentrate on algebraic equations when the night before you dropped a hit of LSD. My world was exploding and no one seemed to notice, or to know what to do. What I can tell you is that had someone simply asked me if I ever thought about my father, or how it felt to be fatherless, if they had in any way helped me to connect the pain with my father loss, they would have unlocked the floodgate to my sad and troubled heart. But no one ever did.

It is humanly inevitable that we will experience loss in our lives. Much of the work of becoming, or of remaining, emotionally healthy, is to sufficiently grieve for our losses as they occur and to not deny the grief when it resurfaces. Unresolved grief festers inside of us and makes us sick. It is often at the core of depression and self-destructive behavior. It is also at the core of violent behavior. In his poem, *Sonnets to Orpheus,* Rilke wrote;

"Killing is a form of wandering melancholy."

Feeling our losses is crucial if we are to be free. From the time that I was a very little girl and accepted the world's mandate that I should forget that I had ever had a father, until I was thirty years old, I did not ever think about him. I never in anyway related the ongoing problems that I had with what had happened to me as a baby. Other people had fathers. I did not. End of story.

In elementary school, when Father's Day came around, the teacher would help the other children make cards for their fathers. I can see myself, off in the corner at a table by myself, coloring in a book or some other activity that had nothing to do with fathers. I can see that child now and I feel so sad for her. She just thought that there was something terribly wrong with her.

Then, when I was thirty, for the first time I loved a man deeply enough to have my heart broken by him. The grief was unbearable. It felt so much deeper than just grief about the ending of that relationship. I wrote in my journal, *Is this what it felt like when my father died?*

For the next several years the only place I would voice these thoughts was in my journals. There, I started to connect my depression to my daddy trauma. By writing the words on the page, I was able to keep the injunction of silence, while trying to find a way to find my truth about my father.

The next shift happened when I decided to write a paper for college on loss and bereavement in childhood. I began reading about early childhood loss. I was finally ready to break the code of silence that had been placed upon me as a child, and for the first time in twenty-six years, I asked my mother about my father.

I wrote to her in Kentucky, explained that I felt that my depression was rooted in my relationship with him, and asked her ten very specific questions. She replied, and I used her answers to my questions in my paper. In answer to question number seven (I have no record of the question,)

"This is another hard one. I had to work. I knew he might go anytime. When I was at work and the phone would ring it would just scare me to death. I had that dread on my mind all the time. I knew he was going to die. You were all I had left and I never turned away from you. I think that having you is all that kept me going. I just felt like a part of me died too."

And who was it that she thought would call her? I was alone with my father. Now perhaps you have a better idea of the level of neglect I suffered. This was the same mother who, in response to my question about how he could lift me out of my crib after his surgery when the doctor had told him to lift nothing heavier than a pencil, she replied "I really don't know."

As I read my mother's letter, the floodgate of grief that had been held back since I was in infant broke open. I cried like my heart was breaking in two, overwhelmed with sadness; my own, my mother's, my father's. Part of me wanted to detach from it, like it wasn't really my experience, that I couldn't claim it. But for the first time I rejected that part as being what wasn't real. The grief for my father was real and it was mine.

In his third volume on *Attachment and Loss*, John Bowlby describes healthy mourning;

"The successful effort of an individual to accept both that a change has occurred in his external world and that he is required to make corresponding changes in his internal, representational world, and to reorganize and perhaps to reorient his attachment behavior accordingly." (16)

Because, as in my case, an infant does not have the ability to process information, and cannot therefore reorganize effectively, this leads to what Bowlby terms "failed mourning." He states;

"The processes of mourning can thus be likened to the processes of healing that follow a severe wound or burn. Such healing processes, we know, may take a course which in time leads to full, or nearly full, function being restored; or they may, on the contrary, take one of many courses each of which has as its outcome an impairment of function of greater or lesser degree." (17)

We never stop mourning our most significant losses. It's not just that I needed my father when I was thirteen-months-old and he died. I needed him at five and eighteen and thirty. I need him today. Even as I write this, I remember myself through all the stages I lived, and see how very alone and in need of a father I was, and I mourn. I reach back in time to who I was, I hold her in my arms, and I let her cry for her daddy. The grief is real, it's just that I can't quite remember the face of the man I am grieving for. He was my daddy, the only one I ever knew.

In a book titled, *The Search for the Real Self,* James Masterson cites the work of Bowlby;

"Reflecting on Bowlby's findings and applying them to my adolescent and adult patients, I realized that there were strong parallels between the mourning process and the defenses it produced in Bowlby's subjects and what my own patients were going through. I came to recognize that when my patients go through a separation experience that they have been defending themselves against all their lives, they seem to react just like Bowlby's infants in the second stage of despair. The separation brings on a catastrophic set of feelings, which I have called abandonment depression." (18)

To suffer trauma is to suffer loss; the loss of other people or of our own abilities or of innocence. To be traumatized is to experience the world as not a safe place, for however long the trauma takes to happen, be it five minutes or a lifetime. When I began to feel my grief about my father, that is when I began to heal.

In my work as a counselor, I have increasingly integrated grief and loss work, both with individuals and in group. I do not believe that, this capacity, to simply be with someone in their grief, is possible unless you have begun to work through your own unresolved grief.

Sometimes, all my patients and clients needed was for me to be able to be with them while they felt their grief. It is not easy to do this. We want to run from it. Or, we think we need to fix it; give empty platitudes, say that it could be worse, deny it, medicate it; anything other than sit there with a forty-year old mentally ill man who will know nothing but an institution for the rest of his life, who had dreams of being a rock star and is now wetting his pants. What else is there to do sometimes but be there to witness to someone's pain?

Several years ago I worked with juvenile felony offenders in Cincinnati. One evening I told them we were going to work on grief and loss in group. I had them arrange their chairs in a circle. At that time, we had seven black and three white teens, ranging in age from fourteen to seventeen.

A rivalry was developing between the two eldest young black men who I will call Lawrence and Peter. I began by giving the group paper and asking that they make a list of all the significant losses in their lives. They looked at me with puzzled expressions; one of them asked,

"What do you mean, like people who died?"

"Yes," I explained, "but other losses too. Something that was important that you lost . . . it could be a pet, or a good friend who moved away, or the loss of innocence."

They each became very serious and worked on their lists for about ten minutes. I then had them take turns reading their lists. The group was very quiet and attentive, really paying respect as each loss was read.

I shared with them some about my father, and some of the other losses I've experienced. I told them that I believe that much of what is wrong with our world is that we suppress our sadness and that so much male violence and rage is a cover up for unresolved grief.

After we talked for a while, I excused them for a break. After they had all got up and left, Lawrence was still sitting beside me, very quiet, holding back tears. He said,

"Do you think we could just end group now? I need to go to my room." I asked why. "I was looking at Peter. You know he looks just like my best friend who got killed last year."

Not really believing that he would, I asked if he thought he could share that with the group. He remained in his seat as the others came back to the room and sat down. He turned to Peter, with tears still in his eyes, and said,

"I was thinking man, you look just like my best friend who got killed last year, the one I was just talking about."

Any hostility Peter had been feeling towards Lawrence melted in that instant. As they continued to share, we all realized that each one of them had someone significant in their lives who had been killed or committed suicide in the previous two years. I was no longer sitting with a group of hardcore young criminals. I was sitting with a sensitive group of young men who felt bonded in their grief.

Doing grief work is not the same as doing regression work. By regression work I mean a process of going back to memories of earlier traumas in order to attempt to heal the emotional pain that is bound there. There are now many different approaches for doing regressions.

Grief is the feeling of sadness attached to the trauma and loss. Our hearts get broken. I can't imagine how a heart can get mended together again without tears. Because I do not yet have conscious memories of witnessing my father die, my connection to it is the feeling of grief.

When I first realized, at the age of thirty, the necessity of mourning my father if I was to ever be whole, there were times I would be consumed by grief. I didn't ask anyone's permission or try to explain it. It was the grief the world had insisted I didn't feel, and I was not going to let anyone intrude upon it.

I would look at the photograph of my father holding me a few weeks before he died and feel the grief and weep. It was this process of connecting to the grief that brought me out of complete dissociation. Although I have slipped in and out since then as conditions become too stressful, I've never again been buried that far within myself.

As the process of mourning became more familiar and my instinct became stronger about it, I then started connecting with the grief as the anniversary of his death or his birthday approached. Once, I was home alone watching television without even realizing it was Veterans Day. A program came on commemorating World War II veterans. As those soldiers on the screen stood at attention while the bugle sounded, I stood up for my father, and all alone with my grief, I cried as though my heart would break.

I believe that when we are hurting in life and the hurt doesn't go away, that there are probably losses to be examined. It is not enough to start with yesterday. Yesterday your relationship ended and you feel angry and abandoned; but what was the original abandonment? Yesterday you found out a friend is dying of cancer and you don't go see her because it hurts too much; don't turn from it. Let your grieving heart open you up to all your losses. Your heart will become tender and wise.

When it hurts too much, get down on your knees and ask God (in whatever way you are able to conceive of God) to help you bear the pain and know what to do.

And then, if you still feel a need for others to support you through this, let your heart guide you to the right others. If you are addicted and co-dependent, seek out 12-step meetings and fellowship. You may find some real comfort in a bereavement group. Find a therapist or other practitioner whose way of working resonates with what you want for yourself. Make an agreement with a trusted friend to serve as co-counselors, which means you structure in a regular meeting time when you each take a turn being a witness to the other and offering what help you can. Make an appointment to meet with a chaplain or other clergy member.

If you are living out your days in a state of emotional numbness and depression, there may be something you need to mourn. I once had a client from Germany who was addicted to heroin and very depressed. The first time we talked, she told me her father had died when she was a baby and that it was because of her.

She then explained that he was in the army and had come home for a visit. She was ill with a deadly virus. Her father got it and died, and she survived. She opened up to me about this because I had on my desk the picture of my father holding me a few weeks before he died.

She became teary as she talked. It was so obvious how much of her present state was rooted back there with her father. When I asked if she had ever worked on that, she replied that she had not. I did not dwell on it, but let her know that anytime she wanted to talk to me about it, I was there. The last time I saw her she sadly shook her head and told me she was already too sad, and she couldn't allow herself to think about what had happened so long ago in Germany.

What I notice as I travel around the United States is how many people are on antidepressant medication, and how few people openly cry or express sadness. It is becoming far less stigmatized to say you are on medication for depression than it is to say you are feeling sadness about your grandmother who died last year or your impending divorce.

As our collective losses and traumas become too frequent and overwhelming, it gets harder to even identify what the bad feelings are about. But for me, I can't imagine that there is any other solution than to keep trying to name the demons that haunt us.

The term *anaclitic depression* was first coined in 1946 by Rene Spitz to describe what he was seeing in institutionalized infants;

"Anaclitic depression was originally described as a psychiatric disturbance in infancy which results from maternal deprivation in the second half of the first year of life. (Spitz 1956) The original description states; "If the nursing staff reports a sudden development of changed behavior in the child without demonstrable organic disease and if this can be correlated to a separation from the child's mother or mother substitute, our suspicion as to the presence of anaclitic depression will be confirmed." (19)

Anaclitic is derived from the Greek word, *anaklitos* (leaning upon.) A related term to describe an infant's inability to take in nutrients and therefore to thrive is *marasmus*. Of course, both of these conditions are related.

This is why the field of neurobiology is so pertinent to the understanding of prenatal and infant trauma. An infant doesn't say to herself *I am so depressed because my mother has left me and so I don't feel like eating today.* These very complex conditions are happening deep within the cells and chemistry of that infant's brain and central nervous system. In my own research I am working on looking at the relationship between early cell death and pathology that develops later in the form of suicidality and self-destructive behavior. In other words; how is cell death related to self death? This is my formulation, first published here in this book.

We are familiar with Charles Darwin's idea of *survival of the fittest.* But he was referring to a genetic tendency that occurs over generations. Anyone who has raised animals understands the concept of the *runt of the litter.* This is the animal in multiple births who doesn't thrive because it is smaller and weaker, possibly very ill. Often the mother rejects the runt. It is easy to understand how that occurs; the sickly little runt is not allowed to take the resources of the others in order for the rest of the litter to thrive.

I witnessed this first-hand with goats. I was working on a goat farm a few years ago. A very young female goat had been placed in with the larger yearlings. The first time I saw her I said something to the owner about how sick and puny looking she was. He told me that her mother had been given antibiotics before they knew she was pregnant, and he thought this might have been why she was so unhealthy.

When I fed them I observed what happened. I put hay and corn in their enclosure. They would all come running for it, including the little goat, who certainly needed it more than the others. The larger goats would simply push her out of the way. And the look on her face was heart-breaking. She wasn't upset with them. It was as though she were saying *Alright, you know what's best and I know I can't eat the food.*

That little goat had no more of a conceptual understanding of her diminished role than a human infant suffering marasmus. Something in her very cell structure was programmed to starve and then die.

This correlates with Allan Schore's description of conservation-withdrawal in his book; *Affect Dysregulation and Disorders of the Self;*

"As opposed to sympathetically driven "fight-flight" active coping strategies, parasympathetically mediated passive coping mechanisms expressed in immobility and withdrawal allow for conservation-withdrawal, the capacity that improves survival efficiency through inactive disengagement and unresponsiveness to environmental input in order "to conserve resources." (20)

Do I experience this in myself? You bet I do. The first time I experienced myself going semi-catatonic was in Chicago at the age of nineteen. There have been other situations since then when I felt very threatened in my relationships or environment and I began to shut down. I withdraw beyond the reach of others and go very deep within myself. My breathing slows, I don't want food, I feel horribly sad and estranged, and unable to respond to others in a normal way. It feels as though I am conserving my own internal energy until the crisis has passed.

When I was about eight, I had this sort of fantasy where I would imagine myself opening a trap-door and going down a long shaft into a basement where there was no other life. Just me in the darkness. I didn't experience that as fearful. Aloneness meant safety. The danger was up there where the other humans were. As an adult, I am reclusive, guarded, defensive, and hypervigilant. I often say of myself that I love humanity as a whole, but can't tolerate most humans. This is what I have said of myself for a long time, and then I read what Stephen Johnson wrote; "The hated child may be one who loves mankind but twists away almost automatically from the closeness required in an ongoing love relationship." (21)

You might ask, how can this woman say she is whole when she suffers so much that seems to imply otherwise? Because, wholeness is found in not being at war against my real self, the self who was made from the environment of my early environment. I know that my essential nature is to be reclusive and guarded. I have endured myself for sixty years now. No one or nothing splits me off from me any longer. If Carl Jung met me, he would agree that I am not good, but I am whole.

My heart is continually being broken by the world. But because of my faith, and some of the wonderful people who have inhabited my life, I am able to let my broken heart be a tender and safe place for others. And, my heart is a tender and safe place for my own true self. That is wholeness.

Margaret Mahler wrote in *The Psychological Birth of the Human Infant; Symbiosis and Individuation;*

"In another case the symbiotic relationship was unsatisfactory for different reasons. The mother of the little boy was depressed during his early infancy. He was her third child and she was rather overburdened. They lived on modest circumstances and crowded quarters. Shortly after the birth of this child, the mother's father, with whom she had had a very close relationship, died. Furthermore, her older child had a serious accident when her third child was only a few months old. The combination of all these circumstances made the mother inadvertently ignore her new child. He was bottle fed, and often fed with his back toward mother. In general, she avoided eye contact with him." (22)

If we want to know who we are as adult beings, we need to look, as closely as we can, at our beginning. That is true for all of us. What are the hidden clues to lead us back to our true self? The circumstances of our infancy might be very different than it was for our other siblings. Adoptees have a particularly difficult time in deciphering what their early life was.

There is a woman in my life who was given up for adoption at birth. Her mother was rejected by the birth father in favor of his legal wife, so we can assume the mother was heart-broken and depressed during pregnancy. The newborn was placed in two separate foster placements before she was six-weeks-old and removed from both because of neglect and/or abuse. The couple who adopted her had been unable to conceive for several years, and then the mother conceived two months after they adopted the infant. The adopted daughter grew up feeling that her younger sister was favored by the mother, without being told she was adopted until she was ten.

What do you believe the prognosis would be for someone who suffered such a traumatic beginning? When we are looking at such severe early trauma and disruption in human bonding, the damage can more accurately be described as neurological and not psychological. It is in the 'hard wiring' of the brain. To understand this, it is the field of neurobiology that has provided the information we need to decode early life.

And at the very core of the psychological work we need to do lies the grief. We must allow the full knowledge of the grief for the loss of the birth parents, the grief for being abused, the loss of innocence, the loss of our birthright to be cared for as a newborn.

Often, when I explain about my own abandonment trauma due to my father's illness and death, someone will ask about my anger. "Have you gotten in touch with the anger?" But for myself (and I have been doing this work for thirty years) there is no anger to be found. There is simply sadness.

A more accurate explanation may be that I have had a lifetime of suppressing my rage because to allow it would be to risk my life. In Stephen Johnson's book, *Characterological Transformation; The Hard Work Miracle*, I find so much that explains me to myself. In particular, his description of the *hated child* or *schizoid* character structure;

"To an even greater extent than with the terror, there is usually a denial and avoidance of the emotion of anger and rage. In infancy, the destructive rage would risk the destruction of the caretaker and therefore the infant himself and could provoke the caretaker's destructive retaliation. Thus, the repression of this emotion is life-preserving. What is encountered, then, in the adult patient, is typically an avoidance or withdrawal from conflict, an inability to get angry or to face anger in others, and the propensity to express it, if at all, in passive-aggressive withdrawal. The hated child has learned to leave rather than fight back and feels that anger is useless and accomplishes nothing. Very often the hated child denies completely his own anger and idealizes and spiritualizes his own loving nature." (23)

For many years now I have accepted that I fit into what is termed personality disorder in the psychiatric nomenclature. I claim this label with pride. To know that I was so deeply damaged by my earliest relationships, and to know the level of deep healing I have achieved, is reason enough to feel proud of myself. Johnson's research to understand the very early trauma and the schizoid experience that evolves from it will continue to help me understand my own characterological make-up for the remainder of my life. He writes;

"But we know that many human infants have been unwanted, and those who have been wanted on a conscious level are not always wanted on a less-conscious level. Furthermore, many parents who think they want children find out differently when the full impact of the totally dependent human being is thrust upon them, when circumstances change, and when their resources to deal with the reality of an infant are much less than expected." (24)

Imagine my mother and father's reality. They probably did want me, and experienced some joy at my birth. But then the reality of having a real infant set in. I believe that my mother returned to work as a waitress very soon after my birth, leaving my morbidly-ill father to tend to me. His resources diminished in proportion to my growing needs to be cared for. His resentment of my needs, his anguish at my crying, his torment in responding to me, did in fact result in a hated child syndrome deep within my psychological and neurobiological being. As Johnson so aptly puts it, "The hated child's experience is: "My life threatens my life."

And this is the state I have found myself in most of my life; that I simply do not feel I have the right to even exist. The world will allow me to exist only if I take from it just enough to survive, and give back, constantly, unflinchingly, with no, or very little, concern for my own needs.

"The schizoid character develops from the environment's negation of the organism's right to be. This negation of the infant's very right to live is believed to occur before or shortly after birth. As a result, the child cannot achieve an adequate symbiotic attachment and, overwhelmed by this environmental response and his organismic reaction to it, he develops a characterological adaptation on the basis of extremely primitive ego abilities and defenses." (25)

This negation of self is directly related to a sense of shame; the sense that, instead of "I make mistakes" we feel "I am the mistake." John Bradshaw deals extensively with what he terms "toxic shame." He states that "Shame is internalized when one is abandoned."

Abandonment does not only occur when one's caretakers die or leave, but whenever they abandon you by not appropriately responding to your normal developmental needs. Physical and psychological abuse, incest, deprivation, emotional violation of one's boundaries (emotional incest) these are all forms of abandonment.

Bradshaw writes, "What I discovered was that shame as a healthy emotion can be transformed into shame as a state of being. As a state of being shame takes over one's whole identity. To have shame as an identity is to believe that one's being is flawed, that one is defective as a human being." (26)

Shame results from experiencing or witnessing traumatic events in childhood but not being allowed to ask questions or express sadness or rage. We then illogically infer (thinking in early childhood is not logical) that we caused the bad things to happen. Of course, the greater the need for secrecy the greater the degree of subsequent shame. This is only one of the reasons why incest is so damaging.

Shame demands that we destroy ourselves, insisting that we don't deserve to live. There is always an element of rage in self-destruction. We may stand for a moment with a dagger poised in our hand to lash out at the world, but then the dagger turns and, ultimately, it is our self we murder.

How tragic for those of us who are shame-bound that often the only release is through behaviors that create more shame. This is the addictive cycle. Something happens that triggers emotional pain and shame, then instead of facing it, we go on an addictive binge, which causes more pain and shame. Our lives become a downward spiral.

When we stop acting out, the pain we have been trying so desperately to avoid hits us full-force. This is when the hard work of recovery begins. Bradshaw writes;

"The most powerful way that our shame defenses crumble are through actual pain and suffering. Pain is a teacher that we can't argue with. Our defenses are there to cover up the pain. Their purpose is to avoid suffering. When we start to experience suffering and pain that are greater than the pain we are trying to avoid, the walls start tumbling down." (27)

When I was a little girl, I did believe that I was somehow responsible for my father's death. The grown-ups in my life refused to engage with me about any of it. At the age of three I asked why he had died. And then, their refusal to understand my need to engage with them, silenced me so completely and reinforced the belief that I had done something wrong. My questions caused my mother pain. So I stopped asking.

There is a photograph taken of me when I was about five on Memorial Day. Every year they would take me to visit my father's grave in the veteran's section of the cemetery. There is a small flag on a stick next to the grave, and they have me 'posed' with my hand gently on the flag. My face is a study in dissociation.

Allan Schore writes with great depth about shame and its relationship in affect regulation with the primary caretakers in infancy. He writes;

"Clinical observers note that failures of early attachment invariably become sources of shame, that impairments in the parent-child relationship lead to pathology through an enduring disposition to shame, and that this results in chronic difficulties in self-esteem regulation found in all developmental psycho-pathologies. If an attachment figure frequently rejects or ridicules the child's requests for comfort in stressful situations, the child develops not only an internal working model of the parent as rejecting but also one of himself as unworthy of help and comfort.

(Bretherton 1985.) This precludes access to interactive regulation at times of emotional crisis." (28)

My entire infancy was a stressful situation. Is it any wonder that a pervasive sense of shame has been with me for as far back as my memories go? When I was younger, there was shame attached to my addictive, acting-out behaviors. In that sense, shame is an emotion of socialization, pointing out to us why we should correct behavior that is harmful to others. But my shame is so much deeper than all that. It is embedded in my source relationships with my father and mother. It is the very stuff I am made of, and it does permeate all my relationships and interactions.

Primarily through my work in 12-step fellowships, I have come so far in healing my toxic shame. I no longer allow others to shame me, I have much better objectivity about looking at the shame within myself, and I do not behave in ways that are self-destructive. But still, the shame is somehow always with me. And alongside the shame is the ever-present awareness that human beings are not, and never will be, a source of comfort for me. It is a lonely existence.

But the reward for all this hard work is that I have an exquisite ability to be here for myself. I have learned to be my own father and mother, best friend and therapist. I feel a deep honor for my own being and all she has gone through. My adult self holds my infant self in a loving and gentle embrace that gives her a feeling of protection that she never had before. I cannot make all the bad feelings go away, but I can hold her and love her while she goes through them. She has a broken heart and always will. But it is a heart encircled in wholeness.

CHAPTER THREE
Science
Trauma and the Brain

"At its peak rate late in pregnancy, the developing brain is producing one hundred thousand nerve cells per minute. The brain will contain ten billion nerve cells by the time of birth. The formation of these cells requires information from the genetic code housed within the dividing cells. The brain also draws on information from the fetus' own environment and activites." (29)

This was taken from a book by Peter Nathanielsz, titled, *Life Before Birth; the Challenge of Fetal Development.* This was one of the books I had on my shelf a few years ago when I was working with teens who had been cited for alcohol and drug use.

In one of my groups I had four seventeen-year-old men. We had spent a few weeks talking about the brain and how it is affected by stress, violence, and drugs. They had really started to grasp the importance of understanding their brains and appreciating the risks they were taking with drug use.

I was trying to impress upon them why the grownups in their lives were wanting them to make different choices. I said,

"Just think what it might feel like someday in the future if you found out your own child was taking drugs."

One of them, a soft-spoken Mexican boy who I will call Alan, said,

"That someday might be pretty soon." He then said he had gotten a girl pregnant. The other boys immediately became very juvenile around it.

"Hey man, you got a girl knocked up! . . . You going to marry her or what?"

I listened for a minute and then got serious, reminding them about how the brain originally forms and is influenced by the mother's environment. A light came on in the expectant father's eyes. I let it go for the time being. When we met again the following week, I started group by telling them I had brought something for them to look at. I handed one of them a framed picture I have showing a newborn being cradled in her father's hands with a quote by Suzanne Arms which reads;

"If we hope to create a non-violent world where respect and kindness replace fear and hatred, we must begin with how we treat each other at the beginning of life. For that is where our deepest patterns are set. From these roots grow fear and alienation . . . or love and trust."

I asked them to remain silent until they had passed the picture around the circle and each read what it said. They did so, really taking in the baby's sweetness and vulnerability. I talked about Alan's relationship with his baby's mother and how important it was to treat her with respect. I suggested that he help her stress level by being clear and honest with her about accepting responsibility toward their unborn child. There seemed to be a new awareness in him that he was already a father and that it began when his baby was conceived.

I picked up Nathanielsz' book and read something about fetal development. After this, we moved on to another topic. A few minutes later I looked over at Alan. He was looking at a drawing of a fetus in the book I had read from. He was totally absorbed and I believe for the first time understood that he had made a human being who already needed him to be sane and healthy, and to be supportive to the mother who was carrying it.

There is nothing more important to teach our teenagers than the knowledge they need to prepare them for the most crucial role they will ever fill, that of mothers and fathers. But, we seem to still be stuck where we were when I was young. We think if we talk to them about parenting we are endorsing them being sexually active.

I was fifteen the first time I got pregnant and then miscarried. No one, before or after, talked to me about being sexually active, or birth control, or what it felt like to lose my baby. Two years later I was pregnant again, and this time delivered a beautiful baby girl who is now my forty-two-year-old daughter. Four years later I gave birth to my beautiful son.

When I was a girl, several of my friends also had babies before they were sixteen. One of them wore three girdles to hide her pregnancy from her parents. Her baby was born with water on the brain and blind, mercifully dying when it was one.

Another friend took LSD during her pregnancy. I said something to her about it and she replied,

"What do I care? I'm giving it up for adoption anyway."

Knowing about how the unborn baby develops is not what will make teenagers go out and have sex. It's their sexual urges that will make them to that. Acquiring knowledge about the complicated and precise development of the fetal central nervous system is what will instill in them a reverence for life, and an understanding that sexual urges should not result in a baby whose parents aren't ready to care for it. This doesn't just apply to teenagers, but to all of us.

How a mother feels about being pregnant and having a baby is the first environmental factor that effects the unborn baby's development. Her attitudes, stress level, ability to feel joy, sense of safety, all are translated into internal chemistry that then influences and help create the fetus' internal chemistry. They are separate beings; yet the same being. There is, right from conception, an exquisite system of communication going on within and between these two (or more if there are multiple babies.)

The chemicals that carry messages throughout the brain and body are called neurotransmitters. They are made of proteins which are made from amino acids. The proper balance of these chemical messengers is what determines how we function emotionally and mentally. Both while we are in the womb, and then after we are born, being deprived of even one essential amino acid can radically change the way we think and feel. Balanced mothers are what make balanced babies.

After birth, it is how the baby is cared for, and the emotional health of its primary caretakers, that is the most essential to its development. In my case, my father was my primary caretaker during most of my waking hours.

Our relationship with the people who inhabited our early environments is, in fact, what makes us. The work of Allan Schore has been a tremendous help in my desire to understand this for myself. In fact, every line in his books seems to describe my own traumatized infant brain to me. Dr. Schore's work has provided to me the manual for my very complex operating system. He writes;

"There is now widespread agreement that the brain is a self-organizing system, but there is perhaps less of an appreciation of the fact that the self-organization of the developing brain occurs in the context of a relationship with another self, another brain. This other self, the primary caregiver, acts as an external psychobiological regulator of the "experience-dependent" growth of the infant's nervous system, whose components are rapidly organizing, disorganizing, and reorganizing in the brain growth spurt of the first two years of life." (30)

The most precious gift that parents and caretakers can give to a child is to continually work on their own emotional, physical, and spiritual health. It is out of a state of health and sanity that we automatically know what is the right thing to do for our child's well-being. The healthier we are, the healthier our relationship with them will be, and this is what largely determines the quality of their relationships with others.

When we realize that biological and spiritual life is complex and multifaceted, we begin to understand that if we are too extreme in one area it may throw us out of balance in some other area. We can become so obsessed with getting the right nutrients that we develop anxiety in ourselves and our families about eating. The anxiety then causes an overproduction of stress hormones which then deplete our nutrient reserves.

If we are already feeling some balance in our lives, then we are able to minimize the level of trauma we experience from the stressors we encounter. Two of the primary brain structures that play a role in traumatic reactions are the locus ceruleus and the amygdala. When we feel threatened in some way, the locus ceruleus becomes over-activated, sending a danger signal to the amygdala. The amygdala somehow stores memories of past danger.

With each successive threat, be it physical or psychological, there are more fear-based memories stored in the amygdala, and other parts of the brain and body. The current threat triggers prior feelings of helplessness and panic. This is why panic attacks are often brought on by being in the same circumstances that brought on prior attacks.

When trauma happens to the physical organism, there is scarring, or broken bones, or some other more or less permanent change. When the trauma is psychological, the enduring effect that it leaves is in the internal communication system within the mind and body. This kind of "scarring" is no less real, just harder to define.

With a physical trauma, it is obvious how crucial it is to treat it as soon after the incident as possible. Bones need to get reset, wounds stitched and bandaged, antibiotics given to prevent infection. This is equally true of psychological trauma. The energy that gets bound up in the trauma needs to be released. We need to talk about it, cry, express anger, pace around the room, get a massage or other body work, breathe deeply, go for a run, get a hug.

Unfortunately, traumas often do not get released, but instead get repressed and compounded. The younger we are when the trauma occurs the more powerless we are to defend ourselves physically or psychologically, or to find appropriate ways to release the energy.

Candace Pert, in *Molecules of Emotion*, writes;

"My research has shown me that when emotions are expressed (which is to say that the biochemicals that are the substrate of emotion are flowing freely) all systems are united and made whole. When emotions are repressed, denied, not allowed to be whatever they may be, our network pathways get blocked, stopping the flow of the vital feel-good, unifying chemicals that run both our biology and our behavior. This, I believe, is the state of unhealed feeling we want so desperately to escape from. Drugs, legal and illegal, are further interrupting the many feed-back loops that allow the psychosomatic network to function in a natural, balanced way, and therefore setting up conditions for somatic as well as mental disorders." (31)

It is these "feel-good" chemicals, particularly endorphins and serotonin, that trauma sufferers are deficient in. Endorphins (endogenous morphine) have the same properties as morphine and other opiates; they cause euphoria and analgesia, meaning they take away all physical and emotional pain. Serotonin is the chemical most closely associated with depression. When it is too low we feel depressed and not emotionally balanced. Anti-depressants do not create serotonin; they cause what existing serotonin we have to circulate in the brain longer.

In the early 1970's, Pert made a discovery that had a major impact in the field of neuroscience. She isolated a molecule on the surface of cells in the brain and body that was a receptor for opiates. What this means is that if someone takes an opiate such as morphine or heroin, there is already a receptor for it to bind to. But, how could that be if there weren't a chemical occurring naturally in the brain that was like an opiate? The researchers were then able to identify a neurotransmitter which they came to call endorphin, meaning endogenous morphine (morphine within).

For a year-and-a-half I worked in methadone treatment. I had forty opiate-addicted clients who I saw in private counseling. I also did a grief and loss group. Methadone is a drug made in the laboratory which was designed to help wean heroin addicts off of heroin and other opiates. The reasoning is that by giving someone a controlled amount of methadone every morning you decrease the need for illegal use which often includes dirty needles, risk of incarceration, prostitution, and other addiction-related behavior. This is called harm reduction.

Many of my clients had tragic lives. Some of this was the result of their addiction. But often the addiction was the result of their tragic lives. I would talk to them about brain chemistry, explaining that endorphins are the chemicals our own bodies create that have all the same effects as morphine. More often than not, these clients would tell me that they never had endorphins and that was why they turned to opiates. It was the only way they felt any peace or joy.

For the most part, these clients had not been in therapy before. They had found their therapy and it was called opiates, but it wasn't working anymore. Out of about 300 clients in our clinic, there would be at least one death a week. I had two clients who died. One, an Indian man, died of cirrhosis of the liver. The other, a woman, who I was convinced had Multiple Personality Disorder, overdosed. She would sit in my office and insist she wasn't using. Her drug tests and autopsy report revealed that she was using several substances.

The best I could do for most of these clients was be a compassionate witness to their suffering, and help them find a little joy to replace the suffering. I could elaborate on the stories of trauma I heard, but out of respect for confidentiality, I won't. Like a deep sea diver I went looking for clues to explain their addiction to them, and to me. I found the clues. They were sad, and sometimes horrific.

Working in the substance abuse field has been frustrating for me. Over and over I have been thwarted in my efforts to deal with root causes. Instead, the drug taking is identified as the problem, when it is in fact the symptom of deeper problems. By the time someone has surrendered, mind, body, and soul, to "the system" they have become putty in the hands of one counselor after another, until they have completely lost any sense of their own capacity for self-healing. This business of humans helping humans is messy.

Addiction is an attempt to self-medicate. What is being medicated may be as simple as boredom or feeling awkward in social settings, or as deep-rooted and complex as Post Traumatic Stress Disorder or auditory hallucinations. I am sure there are cases of addiction that aren't caused by underlying problems, I just haven't personally encountered them.

More often than not, the client does not remember the feelings of unease or panic that led them to use drugs in the first place. I had a young female client who went from taking heroin orally to injecting it. She insisted she just did it because all her friends did and then she got hooked. This woman had an older sister she had been very close to who died unexpectedly while they were teens. She had begun using heroin soon after that, but she insisted that she had been able to mourn her sister and let her go. When we examined it further, she remembered how their mother and other family members had continued to be distraught over the death and that she couldn't deal with seeing them in pain. Then, along came heroin.

There is nothing that we take into ourselves that isn't having its effect by acting on the chemistry that's already there. Heroin, crack cocaine, alcohol, marijuana; all substances that either raise the level of neuro-transmitters or depress brain activity in some way. The same is true of addictive activity; gambling, sex, shopping, changes the chemistry already in the brain. Falling in love gives us bursts of endorphins that make the whole world seem brighter, we hear birds singing and smile alot. Getting our heart broken causes endorphin withdrawal and we feel like we've been punched in the stomach.

When we begin to understand our brain and body chemistry, we feel empowered to make choices to help ourselves heal the imbalances. Real healing means supplying the body with nutrients that are the precursors that build the neuro-transmitters, exercising and moving the body like it was meant to be moved, doing the psychological work of straightening out our thinking and relationships to others, finding ways to calm down and get centered like meditation or tai chi. And developing a prayer life.

It is no accident that so much addiction begins in adolescence. We have just left behind the time in our lives when we were completely powerless; infancy and childhood. We venture out into the world and what we thought was normal in our households we suddenly realize wasn't. Traumas begin to surface. Our hormones are raging inside while all around us rages this new, exciting world called adolescence. Everything we had been denied, but watched the grown-ups participate in; drinking, smoking, sex, is now right there in front of us for the taking.

It is quite clear to me now why I became an addict at the age of twelve. I hated the way I felt inside my entire childhood, so lonely and cut off from others, so much repressed grief about my father. In school, I was so painfully shy that even though I almost always knew the answers to the questions the teachers asked, I wouldn't raise my hand because I couldn't bear for the class to turn and look at me. I didn't have any desire to fit into the world I saw around me. I just wanted out, the quickest way I could get there, and that was alcohol, hallucinogenics, marijauna, and sex.

I didn't start with being a social user because it helped bolster my self-confidence. I went right from shy, naïve child to over the edge addiction where I didn't care about anything or anybody, especially myself.

I can hardly remember the years between twelve and seventeen. My heart may have been broken several times, but I was always too numb to feel it. I remember the highlights. Other girls cherish memories of their first kiss, the prom, becoming class president. I remember the suicide attempt, the miscarriage, the running away from home, and never wanting to look in the mirror.

I was filled with pain but turned it inward on myself. Although I loved my big extended Appalachian family, I did not even think about going to any of them to try and talk through what was bothering me. And, they didn't ask. Some of my teachers tried to help by letting me make up exams when I had skipped school or encouraging my artistic talents. But I don't remember any adult ever simply asking me if I had any idea why I was so unhappy.

I left Kentucky at the age of nineteen with my baby daughter and went to Chicago to live in a commune. We would live communally in one place or another for the next six years or so. Those of us who "dropped out" of mainstream society in the 70's had some very good instincts. We knew that we all needed more natural diets, that we needed more cultural sensitivity and love for others, that the environment would be in grave danger if we didn't change our trajectory, that we needed to breastfeed our babies. But, for a young woman as troubled as I was, the consequences of communal living were devastating because of the lack of sexual boundaries. I have paid a very high price for all that "free love."

It was while I was living in Chicago that I went into my first major depression. In that household, there were the adults, all in their late twenties and early thirties. Then, there were our children. Stuck right in the middle was nineteen-year-old me, vulnerable, beautiful, and at times almost catatonic.

I remember lying on my bed, too depressed to eat or speak, and people all around me asking what was wrong. I had sealed myself off very deep inside.

Physiologically, I went into freeze mode. This remained my pattern throughout all the years I was a part of the great communal experiment. In normal development, the ego houses our being, functioning as a protective shell against the world, while allowing us to exist effectively in the world. Its doors and windows open to let the world in, and close when the world intrudes too much upon us.

But when boundaries were violated when we were young, our doors keep flying open, we have no control over our own house. No boundaries . . . open house. Or close up everything, seal ourselves off inside so no one can find us. Let the weeds grow so they think no one's home.

In Chicago, I attended the Art Institute, continuing my passion for art that had started in the 6th grade. From the time I was eleven until I was twenty-two, I completed hundreds of drawings and paintings representing many hours of dedication to my craft. I stopped after my son was born. Somehow, over the years since, all of these pieces of art, pieces of me, have disappeared. I can only account for two paintings. The rest were either destroyed, or given away, or stored somewhere. I have no memory of what happened to them.

The human brain has the capacity to create fine works of art. It also has the capacity to experience so much shame and guilt that it will allow those pieces of art to be destroyed because it doesn't feel worthy to have created them. Within the same brain, there can be the drive to create and the drive to destroy. Feelings of hope and elation can in the next instant turn to hopelessness and despair, without any apparent external stimulus.

The complexity, mystery, and sometimes the horror of human life is generated from processes inside the brain that were put into motion at conception, or before. As the interplay between genetics and environment are seen more clearly, I believe we will begin to see a much more accurate picture of how the brain becomes what it does.

What has been attributed to the genes will be reassessed in light of what is being learned about prenatal and perinatal development. We will not hear as much about "bad genes" and more about "bad neuronal migration."

Understanding the physiology of the brain and body has transformed the way I see myself, and others. Whenever I begin feeling too critical of myself; my mood swings, poor boundaries, stressed relationships, I look at a picture of my father holding me a few weeks before he died. He is very thin and emaciated, barely seems able to hold himself up. I rest there in his arms, the arms that will soon cease to ever hold me again. That baby's life is getting ready to shatter. I look at the picture and forgive myself of everything.

I am also more apt now to talk to clients about what might be going on with them chemically. Instead of saying, "You seem kind of manic today," I might say, "I bet your dopamine level is sky-high today, why do you think that might be?" There is so much less shame in that, and it is empowering to know we can affect our chemistry.

I have found this approach particularly helpful with teens. They so often feel internally out of control due to chemical and hormonal changes. Adolescence usually isn't the time we focus on healthy eating and self-care. And many teens are experimenting with mood-altering substances. To help them understand how adrenaline, serotonin, dopamine, and endorphin affects their moods and behavior, gives them a tool they can use to navigate through life.

This sort of education will not be initiated, or supported by the medical and phamaceutical establishment. There is no money to be made in people eating right, meditating when they're stressed, or doing self-therapy. This education will come from those of us who insist that it is our right as humans to understand the way our brains are formed, how they develop along healthy or unhealthy pathways, and what we can do to heal.

My father had flashbacks of Ploesti. My flashbacks of being his daughter are "emotional flashbacks." I do not have conscious memories, but my brain goes back there, experiencing intense terror, threat, and loss of control.

The process of flashing back is being studied extensively in combat veterans. Scientists at the Minneapolis VA Center and the University of Minnesota, reported these findings in 2010;

"Researchers found a difference between communication in the temporal and parieto-occipital right hemispheric areas of the brain. The temporal cortex, in accordance with earlier findings on the effects of its electrical stimulation during brain surgery, is thought to be responsible for the reliving of past experiences. The findings are something conventional brain scans, such as an x-ray, CT, or MRI have failed to do. Of particular interest to the scientists however is that brains of the sufferers were in this hyperactive state despite no immediate external stimulation, as the trial subjects were purposefully put into a 'task-free state' meaning PTSD sufferers can relive terrifying memories at any moment, regardless of what they are doing." (32)

And it is also true that sometimes flashbacks are triggered by very definite external stimuli. I only have one reference to my father's flashing back that has come from outside my own awareness. My aunt said he was found bailing water out of the bathtub and saying "I'll save you buddy." My cousin said he was shaving at the sink and splashing water out saying the same thing. Either way, the visceral experience of water on his skin and the sight and smell of it triggered the memory of his plane crashing into the sea.

Think about this in your own life. Maybe you have suffered extreme traumatic events. Or less severe traumas, like almost being in a car accident, or someone yelling at you. What triggers your memory of it? Sometimes it might get triggered by something specific. At other times, it comes to consciousness out of nowhere.

I recently was at a friend's house and tried a piece of Christmas candy that had an unusual combination of spices. It was triggering some memory in me. Then I realized the candy smelled like the cologne my uncle wore when I was a child, Old Spice. I was immediately back in time with him and the smell of him as he headed out the door to go to the Moose Lodge. This is a pleasant memory for me as I loved and trusted him. If there had been trauma embedded in the memory, the candy might have triggered a traumatic flashing back.

The difference with traumatic memories is that different areas and structures of the brain are activated, and stress-related chemicals are discharged into the brain. The olfactory bulb in the human forebrain is what processes smell. There are about 10 million olfactory receptor neurons, and the memory of the smell of something is retained longer than memories via other senses.

My work to understand just how damaged I am from the traumatic circumstances of the first year of my life began with the eruption of grief about my father. Then I was compelled to write the paper for college on loss and bereavement. The next major shift came for me as I was working to complete my bachelor's degree in psychology.

I chose to graduate from The Union Institute because the program fit my life, and because Clarissa Pinkola Estes had graduated from Union. Reading her book, *Women Who Run With the Wolves,* gave me permission to be all that I am; an intellectual and scholar who likes to wade in creeks and sing Irish ballads and who had visions of Indian warriors as a child. Her book gave me permission to reclaim my soul.

"It is worse to stay where one does not belong at all than to wander about lost for a while and looking for the psychic and soulful kinship one deserves." (33)

When I enrolled at Union I had already worked as a counselor in the system for fourteen years. My clients and patients were where my real learning came from about all that is human. I didn't need to take a class in Abnormal Psychology; they were my class. My commitment to them fueled my desire to study psychology.

But delving into my own traumatized infant brain would require something more, and that something is the field of neurobiology. At Union, I chose to take Biological Psychology, and because I was working full-time in psychiatric treatment and raising two children, I was allowed to work mostly independently. I wrote two papers; *Anti-Social Personality; Is There a Neural Pathway for Conscicence?* and *The Influence of Traumatic Stress on Brain Plasticity.*

Plasticity is defined by Heinrich Reichert this way;

"The notion that the nervous system is a rigid, hard-wired functional unit, and is therefore more like a collection of integrated circuits than living tissue, does not correspond to reality. Many regions of the brain can change structurally and functionally, depending on sensory experience. Certain neuronal systems are even critically dependent on sensory information from the environment to become correctly configured during postnatal development. The mechanisms mediating this developmentally based plasticity can remain active long after the early postnatal phase. The stability of fully developed synapses is constantly affected by experience, as are some of the neuronal connectivity patterns, even in the mature brain." (34)

Reading the neuroscientists was like hearing a beautiful melody played on a violin, straight to my heart and mind. It was music after a lifetime of discordant notes and chaotic noise. Simply by reading the theorists and then writing the papers, my brain began to configure itself in a new and more whole way. They validated for me that I am not crazy and wrong. The trauma I shared with my father has everything to do with the woman I became. They gave me permission to never give up searching for my lost father in the recesses of my mind and soul. And their commitment to our shared field of research reassured me that I would never be quite so alone again.

What we refer to as character or personality is deeply imprinted from our very beginning. Our fundamental personality only changes through extreme life-changing events, physical trauma to the brain, and/or very very hard work. We can, in a sense, re-program our brains and central nervous system.

Suicidality, addiction, and other forms of self-destructive behavior are increasingly being viewed in terms of inter-uterine life, birth trauma, and neonatal development. In 2007, an article was published in *Biology of the Neonate (Can Adverse*

Neonatal Experiences Alter Brain Development and Subsequent Behavior?);

"Self-destructive behavior in current society promotes a search for psychobiological factors underlying this epidemic. Perinatal brain plasticity increases the vulnerability to early adverse experiences, thus leading to abnormal development and behavior. Although several epidemiological investigations have correlated perinatal and neonatal complications with abnormal adult behavior, our understanding of the underlying mechanisms remains rudimentary. Models of early experience, such as repetitive pain, sepsis, or maternal separation in rodents and other species have noted multiple alterations in the adult brain, correlated with specific behavioral phenotypes depending on the timing and nature of the insult. The mechanisms mediating such changes in the neonatal brain have remained largely unexplored." (35)

In my capacity as an educator I have twice been contacted by men who were circumcised as newborns. Both men reported to me that they felt no one in their lives seemed to understand how this had affected them. They both reported feelings of extreme anxiety with no apparent external triggers. They generally felt unsafe in the world, and had anger about the procedure being done to them as infants.

Our brains store traumatic experience. It is that simple. The mechanisms on a cellular level for how this happens are incredibly complex. By some process that we are just now beginning to understand, a feeling state such as "I don't have the right to exist" gets translated into our very molecules. Those molecules then are programmed for a lifetime of acting this out in our behavior.

An infant who develops in an atmosphere of abuse and neglect develops an entirely different brain system than an infant who is well cared for. My brain is not the same as the brain of someone who did not suffer stress in infancy.

The implication of this is far-reaching and profound. There are, no-doubt, many people who have undiscovered traumas going back to birth and infancy, and who may never have enough information to make the correlation. Those who did suffer early trauma and are doing the work to understand it are truly on the front-line of neurobiology. Freud's term *infantile amnesia* is the last frontier to be explored. Our infant selves have so much to tell us.

CHAPTER FOUR
Dissociation
Where Was I When I Wasn't There?

Most people have experienced dissociation in its mildest form. You get in your car to drive somewhere, your mind is preoccupied with the meeting you are preparing for, and the next thing you know you are there without any memory of having driven there. But if you "come to" a year later without knowing where you've been, or your personality splits into separate personalities, this is dissociation to the other extreme.

In the first instance, the cause is daydreaming or being preoccupied. Part of the mind is going over the speech you are about to give while the other parts are navigating traffic and operating the car. But with the other, more extreme forms, the causes are also extreme.

Each case of Multiple Personality Disorder that I have studied was caused by severe sexual and physical abuse or witnessing violence in childhood. Amnesia is caused by shock or brain injury. Dissociation of the more extreme form happens because awareness would be too painful. The mind has an uncanny ability to protect itself. With lesser traumas the mind employs other defenses; denial, rationalization, projection. If these defenses aren't strong enough to protect the core self then the mind closes off awareness completely.

Although MPD is fairly rare, anyone working in the mental health field needs to have some knowledge of what to look for. Because I had studied it, I was able to recognize it in a female patient in psychiatric treatment in Kentucky. Apparently no one else had even suspected it.

My very first intuition about her case came as I was talking on the phone with the doctor who was referring her from the emergency room at another hospital. He wanted us to admit her for an evaluation. He said that her diagnosis was a seizure disorder and that she had been seen many times in the ER. They were concerned because they were now seeing other behavior. I asked him what they were seeing.

"She goes over to the wall and starts feeling it like there is something on it."

The young woman was brought to our unit. She was in her late twenties, very pretty and timid. I will call her Jane. She came from a very impoverished eastern Kentucky upbringing. She was compliant with whatever we asked her to do. It didn't take long before we witnessed what had been labeled as a seizure disorder. She would sit on her bed and look very "spaced out."

Then she would raise her hand up as though to ward off a blow. We observed her for a few days and tried to help her feel safe. She began opening up to us and telling us about her husband hitting her. On the third day I went into her room and sat next to the bed. I asked her if we could talk about her childhood. I already knew from her case file that when she was twelve she had been removed from the home where she lived with her widowed father. Her mother had died sometime before.

We began talking about what she could remember of the day she and her siblings had been removed from home. She said that she remembered that her sister had said that their father had hurt her somehow. I asked her if he had ever hurt her in anyway. She replied,

"My daddy wouldn't even hurt a fly."

She wasn't able to report much else about her childhood. She told me that she had been sent to a state institution and the name of the town it was in. The next day we sent for the records from the institution. She and her siblings had been removed from home because the father was having sex with his daughters, as were the older brothers. The case history painted a picture of incest and depravity. Several of the children had been diagnosed with either schizophrenia or seizure disorders.

Jane's husband was ready for her to come home and was enraged that we were keeping her. He showed up one day at the nurse's station in the hospital. He could not come to the psych unit unless they buzzed the door open for him. When they refused he kicked a hole in the desk. They called the police and he was taken to jail. Several days later he was released from jail and called from a pay phone threatening to kill us if we didn't release Jane.

The social worker and I located a battered women's shelter in the next county and agreed that we would transport her there. Because her two young daughters were staying with relatives we would first have to pick them up and then drive them all to the shelter. We arranged for a deputy sheriff to follow us there in his patrol car. On the day we did this we put Jane in the back seat, drove to meet the deputy, then picked up the girls and drove Jane and the girls to the shelter. We were in the car with her for about two hours. For that two hours I got a sense of what a battered, terrorized woman feels every moment.

Her husband had a small blue car. She kept jerking around and looking at every blue car that passed saying "There he is!" I was a nervous wreck by the time we reached the shelter.

They called us a few days later to tell us that their psychologist had given her the diagnosis of Multiple Personality Disorder. The next time I heard about her she had gone back home to live with her abusive, alcoholic husband. The little girl inside her who had been defenseless with her incestuous father was now defenseless with her deranged husband.

In my own case, I am not sure what my mind did after I witnessed my father's death, other than become increasingly depressed. As a child I felt sadness and shame and loneliness. But I was there. It wasn't until I was twenty-four that I became fully dissociated for the first time.

The severe depression that I sunk into at the age of nineteen had not lifted when I became pregnant with my son three years later. The circumstances surrounding my pregnancy and the birth only deepened the depression. My son's father had been in a relationship for the six years prior to his involvement with me. They had agreed to live in separate states, but still see each other occasionally. The same month that I discovered I was pregnant, she was told she had cancer and had less than a year to live. As I became more full of the life I was carrying, she was wasting away from chemotherapy and cancer. The last time I saw her alive she had lost all her hair and looked like a skeleton. When my son was three-weeks-old, she committed suicide.

My son's birth was very traumatic. It began as a home birth with all our friends and my daughter there. He was stuck. No one understood that I needed to get to the hospital. I labored all night and the next morning and was then rushed by ambulance to the hospital where I was given an epidural. Instead of being at home with my baby with me, I was drugged and heartbroken with him crying in shock in the nursery. It was horrible. I am just now beginning to understand the impact that had on my bonding with him.

I did not deal with any of this. I was on "automatic" for the next four years. On the outside I'm sure I appeared to be quiet and gentle, with no hint of the deep trouble I was in. Life continued around me; inside I was dying. This is where the line between depression and dissociation gets very blurry for me. Chemically speaking, my serotonin level must have been just about non-existent.

The poet, Sylvia Plath, described her depression as being under a "bell jar." This is what it felt like for me then. I could see and hear life around me, but through a deep fog. Somehow the decision was made that we; my daughter, son, and his father, would move to California to live near some of the other people we had been living with in a communal arrangement.

Once again I was leaving the forest and farms that I loved so much and going to a city. We drove our school bus out there. I had fallen asleep as we approached Los Angeles. I awoke while we were at a gas station downtown. When I looked out on to a scene of nothing but pavement and buildings and people, I think I experienced shock.

I have very few memories of the next year. There was more of the sexual openness that had before caused me to withdraw and become immobilized. My relationship with my son's father became so "open" that I flew right out of it. I knew that I was in deep emotional trouble. I sent him up north with the children and I stayed in southern California for the next nine months.

There is so much pain for me in this that I can barely write the words. I sent my beautiful, blond-haired babies away and spent almost a year roller-skating up and down the boardwalk.

I was in a fugue state. I wasn't there. There was no sense of personal identity. I did not experience emotion. Outwardly, I became more beautiful and more fit than I've ever been in my life. But, inside, there was nothing left.

I took the bus north twice, I believe, to be with my children. Once, it was Christmas and I stayed with them in the truck-camper they shared with their father. There were Christmas lights. I loved my children so much, and I left them again, and I don't know why. Sometime after I returned to L.A. I broke my back roller-skating and was then sexually molested by a chiropractor. I have had back pain and ringing in my ears since then.

The wound that happened that year to me and to my children has never healed, for me or for them. Becoming that dissociated was something that was begun with my father's illness and death, and finally caught up with me in southern California. The day I started to "come to" someone had asked me if I had children. From somewhere far away I heard a voice say yes, and realized it was my own.

Where was I when I wasn't there? I will probably struggle with this question for the rest of my life. Because of the abandonment trauma that my children experienced when I dissociated I continue to feel tremendous grief and guilt about that year.

We do very often wound our children in the ways we were wounded. Parents who were sexually or physically abused can then go on to be perpetrators. Growing up with overly critical parents will often turn us into being too critical of our own children. Parents who themselves experienced extreme neglect will often not have the resources to adequately care for their own children. In my case, I experienced severe abandonment trauma and then went on to abandon my own children.

When I think about where I was when I wasn't there, what comes over me is how it felt to be me as an infant, after my father died. I will never be able to explain to anyone the feeling of the abyss I fell into.

For reasons I don't completely understand, the experience of taking an afternoon nap is so awful for me that I fight taking naps, even if I'm exhausted. When I wake up from a nap in mid-afternoon I awaken to a feeling of dread and doom that is so oppressive it feels as though I will die from it. It is an emotional state that is somehow connected with waking in the middle of the day.

It would make more sense to me if my father had died in the middle of the day. Instead, he died at four o'clock in the morning. I was then taken to stay with some relatives. Could it be that when I awoke from my first nap after I watched him die, the knowledge of what had happened filled my little heart with doom? Could that first shock of awakening be recorded in my brain?

Going deep inside ourselves to do "soul retrieval" is the only way to find our own soul. Where else would it be? That's why others can only try and guide us through it, hold our hand, offer to make dinner while we fall apart. If we want to be whole we must go back down into our memories and dreams and neurosis. We come back up each time holding more and more pieces, and saying,

"Look world, see these pieces. They are me and now I'm going to figure out how to put them back together again."

This is the work that my father couldn't, or wouldn't, do. Instead I was the baby he left behind to sort through his war trauma. Years ago I watched a program on World War II that began with a woman reading a letter which her father had sent to her when she was a child, before he was killed overseas. He wrote about his hopes and dreams for her, how he wanted to come back home to be with her, but if he couldn't, he wanted her to know something about him.

During the first year of my life, as my father struggled with the physical and psychological disease which then killed him, it seems to me that he would have wanted to leave behind a journal or letters for me. How could he have not looked at me every day and felt the need to leave me words; words that I was then unable to comprehend.

It is not possible for those of us who have never been in active combat to understand the level of trauma that veterans, and their victims, experience. That is why countless veterans return from war feeling completely alone with their experience. In my father's case, he wasn't alone. He was there with a baby girl who knew that her survival depended on his ability to respond to my emotional and physical needs. Is it any wonder that I have never in my life felt the experience of being safe?

The authors of a book titled, "*The Trauma of War; Stress and Recovery in Vietnam Veterans,*" present many case histories of veterans who returned from Viet Nam experiencing feelings of "not being all there." The horrors they had participated in or witnessed were so traumatic they couldn't be integrated or worked through. There is now a wealth of data and knowledge about the effects of the Viet Nam War on veterans. The term post-traumatic stress disorder (PTSD) was first used to describe Viet Nam veterans.

"Much of the psychic life of these individuals is devoted to re-experiencing traumatic events, and on an unconscious level these individuals strive to master their traumas by making them come out differently. The altered state of consciousness occurs in the service of this task. Since the disorder is so psychologically painful, many of these individuals sedate themselves with drugs or alcohol. Since at the core of the disorder is a fear of loss of loved ones and friends, these individuals keep distant from those around them to avoid the inevitable pain of departure and loss." (36)

When I read this, I try to imagine what my father's relationship to his infant daughter was? How could he "keep distant" from the baby he was left to care for every day? Certainly he was filled with ambivalence; wanting to experience his love for me but defended against the pain of losing me.

Human relationships are never simple. When there has been severe trauma, relationships become even more complex. Our experience of life is built on the relationships we have with our primary caretakers in our earliest development.

"Veterans of guerilla war, or those immersed in an enemy milieu in ordinary war or concentration camps, have had to endure lengthy periods when primary distinctions between annihilating and non-annihilating objects were profoundly confused and difficult to maintain. Under such conditions primitive distinctions (referable to the 1st year of life as regards the psychic structures involved) between good and bad objects are of immediate, continuous, life-saving importance and are constantly challenged." (37)

During infancy, as I was struggling to develop my own primitive distinctions, my father was struggling to re-establish his. The profound damage this did to my development I am only just now beginning to understand. Relationships have always been full of tension and unease for me. I suppose on the surface I appear to do very well. But underneath I am constantly on guard, knowing that it is only a matter of when, not if, the relationship will begin to hurt.

This is probably the primary reason I became a counselor and an educator. It is just so much more satisfying to be engaged with people about real issues. My level of empathy as a child and young woman was acute. I knew the pain others carried around inside, often not even aware of it themselves. Now I can help others bring the pain out where it can't do so much damage.

We live in a world that is fraught with personal tragedies, global warfare, natural disasters, and child and spousal abuse. Humanity is traumatized. Humanity is the source of most of the trauma. We can no longer insulate ourselves from what happens anywhere on this planet. Either we all find a way towards collective healing, or we will perish.

The extent to which we did not develop in a natural healthy way in infancy and early childhood is the extent to which we must do our work now. People who grow up well, surrounded by psychologically healthy adults, often don't seem to understand what all the fuss is about.

We can allow ourselves to feel very judged by their opinions of our continuing problems. But, people who are healthier are not the only ones who may seem not very supportive of our efforts to heal.

When I first began to do education about prenatal and childhood trauma, I couldn't understand the walls I was coming up against. When we hit those walls it can feel like a trauma in itself. Every time the baby girl inside me needed someone to understand and they didn't, she was hurt all over again. We can protect our inner child by developing the intellectual capability to discern other's reactions to our efforts to heal.

Here are some of the walls I've encountered. Not everyone in these categories behave in this way; but some do.

• People who have done some childhood work and are defended against going deeper. Because they seem savvy about healing, we can feel very shut down by them. Essentially they are saying "I've done my work and I'm threatened by you suggesting there may be more work to be done."

When you are dealing with this just remember that it is no one's place but yours to know if you have more work to do, or at what pace. But also remember that we need to respect their boundaries. They may need to take a break from healing work; it doesn't mean we have to.

• Parents who have raised children. Since there is no such thing as a perfect parent or a perfect childhood, most parents feel guilty about something they did or didn't do. So if you're talking about healing your own infant and childhood wounds you are going to trigger that guilt. This often happens on an unconscious level. They know that being around you brings up sadness in them. What they haven't yet dealt with about raising their children now starts to surface. They remember the time they lost control or got lost in addiction or failed somehow.

• Parents who have adopted children. When a baby or child is adopted the almost magical belief is that whatever damage was done can now be reversed by a loving and stable home filled with comfort. These parents are defended against knowing that they may not be able to undo the harm that has already been done to their child. They create a wonderful fairy land and do not want it disturbed. As adoptive parents begin to understand the inherent issues involved with adopting they can find ways to help their child heal. But, many adoptive parents I've encountered do not want to know that there has been damage that may not be healed in the way they would like it to be.

• Elderly people. Many times I have been disappointed by someone in their later years who seems totally unsupportive of my focus on healing childhood wounds. It may be that because they themselves suffered through so much as a child they think we should just "pull ourselves up by the bootstraps" and stop whining. My parent's generation could not indulge themselves in the same way we do. They feel that it is too late to begin to deal with their own woundedness, so they can't offer much support. I once met a woman in her late 80's who had read an article in the newspaper about my work to heal the trauma of my father's illness and death. She said that when she read the article she thought "What's the big deal . . . she didn't get raped or anything."

• Professionals in the mental health field. There is a very insidious process that has happened whereby those trained in a traditional paradigm believe that psychological healing is their domain. They may not want to know much about how you are taking responsibility to heal yourself. Although I have been helped immensely by knowledge I have gained by some psychotherapists, there are many others who I feel have done more damage than good. Do not treat them as gods. Treat them as adjuncts to your healing. When our source relationships were so dangerous in early life we have to be cautious about how much power we give to any one person. Therapists tend to only be able to help us heal to the depth they are healing themselves.

• Other family members may be very defended against all the digging we do into our family systems. They may prefer that we just leave it alone. Although we may have grown up in the same family and social context, that doesn't mean that our experience was theirs. The order of our birth, our gender, and our personality, all affect the way we grow up. Just because you are ready to look at your childhood doesn't mean they have to be. Be compassionate towards yourself and others in your family who were wounded. If you or other family members were very violated in some way then realize that you are opening up a 'pandoras box' and proceed with caution.

• Our own children. At the age of forty when I first began to uncover the trauma of my infancy, I was certain that my children would be supportive of me. My daughter was then in her early twenties and my son in his late teens. They had grown up with a mother who was not quite all there, and who then shifted into being way too much there. My anxiety level was enormous and I just would not suppress it any longer by pretending to be okay. I wasn't okay and the world was going to know it. They each had their own ways of defending against that intense period in my healing. She traveled around the world and detached herself. He vacillated between being angry with me and then just not wanting to deal with any of it.

These are some of the situations that we may find ourselves in, not understanding why we feel so unsupported and unacknowledged for our attempts to uncover and heal trauma. When this happens, we need to step back and look at what might be happening.

Are we stepping across someone's boundaries? Are we being overly sensitive? In the beginning of recovery there are many obstacles to overcome, some from without, and some from within. Over the course of a lifetime we develop many ways to avoid pain and increase pleasure. Some are fairly benign, like reading romance novels. Others become full-scale addictions that can totally destroy our lives and the lives around us.

When we begin to confront the pain instead of running from it, the internal demons we unleash can be very frightening. This is when we most need to have some support system in place. 12-step programs, support groups, therapists, and good friends can be crucial at this time.

There are obstacles both inside and out. But, we can begin to exchange unhealthy tools for healthier tools. Make a list of constructive alternatives to help through the bad times. Using these tools wisely doesn't mean that we then become obsessed with the new tools instead of the old addictions.

The word addiction is from the Latin term "ad dictum;" to the dictator. If some person place or thing is dictating too much of our lives then we are using it addictively. Healing addictions is about finding balance.

My personal "toolbox" for self-soothing has included; praying, meditating, writing, journaling, exercise, jigsaw puzzles, genealogy, painting, hot baths, and working out my pain on paper. What I mean by that is that sometimes when I cannot write about it or even conceptualize it, I can write it out. For instance, if I'm struggling with feeling too scattered I might take a piece of paper and draw circles representing my major life goals and then see if all my daily activities are fitting in the circles. Or I might make a list of relationships I feel I need to let go of and then burn it in the fire, saying a prayer for those people.

All of the above activities are solitary. They are what I consider to be self-soothing. Because we are such social creatures I think we can become too dependent on others to make us feel good. If we are more able to help ourselves feel good about ourselves, then we can enter into all of our relationships feeling more whole and grounded. Of course the danger here is in isolating too much. It is all a question of balance.

For so many years I played "the good girl." I wanted to be liked, and I was. There wasn't much about me that offended anybody. I was quiet and easy to please. But that façade became too hard to maintain. My survival depended on me breaking out of that mold. If you're going to "find yourself" you can't be looking for the you everybody else wants you to be. You have to look for the you you to need to become.

What I have noticed about people who aren't very evolved themselves is that there is no way to win with them. When we're not doing well they are the first to judge, "Why can't you get it together? Why don't you calm down . . . cheer up . . . take medication?" Then, if we are able to begin succeeding in life, they are so filled with envy they can't acknowledge our success.

I once knew a recovering alcoholic who would say, (referring to himself) "It's none of my business what somebody else's experience of me is." When I first heard him say that my mind went into a spin, trying to figure it out. Then, I got it. Somebody else's experience is really about them more than it can ever be about you. The way they experience you usually has very little to do with who you are.

Healing is about claiming authority over ourselves. We are the one and only person who has been there our entire lives. When all the pieces get dug up from the subterranean depths we have to figure out how to put them together. Others can guide us. They can't be us.

We are on a journey in the company of our own self. That self, moment by moment, chooses a path. If we can begin to be curious and awake enough, we will notice where our life path is taking us and begin to feel like the path we are choosing is leading to more sanity and self-acceptance. The path we are leaving behind us will still be there; behind us.

The experiences that happened to us along the way did shape us. And we will continue to be shaped for the rest of our lives by the experiences that we choose, and by the events that are beyond our control. Finding a greater sense of safety within all the experiences happening around us is not always easy.

Some of us have more stressful lives. Physical illness, poverty, dysfunctional family systems, and addiction all add to stress levels. Some of it is within our control. Much of it isn't. When we allow others to blame us for not matching up to their expectations we create more stress for ourselves.

Allan Schore cites the work of Pierre Janet;

"Furthermore, Janet speculated that dissociation was the result of a deficiency of psychological energy ("la misere psychologique.") Due to early developmental factors, the quantity of psychological energy is lowered below a critical point, and thus individuals with characterological dissociation are deficient in binding together all their mental functions into an organized unity under the control of the self." (38)

And this is exactly what happened to me when I was twenty-four and had first moved to California. Notice the statement that it is the psychological energy that becomes critically lowered. We imagine a depressed person to be depressed not only in mood, but in physical energy. In my case of dissociation, my thinking was not depressed, it simply wasn't there. My physical energy wasn't depressed, for the year that I was separated from my children I was a very serious outdoor roller skater. I worked for a skate company, was an extra in a skate movie, and skated the boardwalk on Venice Beach during every daylight hour I wasn't working. I had become a robot; a young, beautiful, skating robot.

The deficiency was in binding together my mental energies into an organized unity under the control of a self. My self-identity was shattered. Before that time, my primary identity was as a mother to my sweet and good children. During my dissociative episode I was so split off I had no awareness of my children. I never thought about them. Prior to California, they had almost never been away from me, for seven years. There was no sense in me of having an identity that endures over time, defining me to myself and others, has a more-or-less consistent core, and holding me together in a way congruent with my beliefs. I had no beliefs. I had no future. I had no self.

When I try and explain this to my children now I say that my mind shattered. That the extreme trauma I suffered in infancy, combined with my mother's almost total lack of an emotional self, caught up to me on Venice Beach and I split off.

And it was precisely the conditions I had experienced in Chicago living in the commune that brought on this second and more severe dissociative state; an atmosphere of sexual partner swapping. I can remember the exact instant that the split occurred. My son's father was standing at a distance watching me perform some skating feat for a crowd of onlookers. It was as if he had no relationship to me, a total stranger, admiring my beauty but resentful of my detachment from him. My mind could find no meaning, could make no sense of my life. It split.

I have no memory available to me of my children leaving with my son's father to come north. None. Prior to my split, I was a devoted, wise, and loving mother. And then my two children were gone, and I have no memory of it, nor am I able to search for the memory because of the pain that blocks it.

Our decision, made in Pennsylvania, to come to California and to provide our children a better life, was shattered deep within me at the suggestion that we enter into a four-marriage with another couple. This is the closest I can get to describing my dissociation.

But these are only the outward manisfestations of a process that happened deep within the neurobiology of my brain and central nervous system. What is that process? For these explanations I look to the scientists. From a book titled *Neurobiology and Treatment of Traumatic Disscociation: Toward an Embodied Self;*

"The thalamus is a composite of nuclei that receives input from all the senses and disperses information throughout the cortex. The part of the ACC that is functioning abnormally in PTSD has major inputs from subcoritical structures for sensoriomotor integration, emotions, defense, and autonomic regulation mediated by mediodorsal, intralaminar, and midline nuclei and the medial pulvinar of the thalamus. Thus, disrupting the thalamus means disrupting widespread activation throughout the brain, and thus connectivity between different brain regions. This includes both vertical and horizontal integration of brain functioning, ultimately contributing to the breakdown of integrative functioning of the brain under threat." (39)

Myself, and my daughter and son, still suffer from that year I was gone from them. And it's not just that I was living a few hundred miles away. There are parents who create a co-parenting situation from long distances that do not impact their children in a traumatizing way. The real damage for my children comes in their knowing that their mother went from being totally available to them, to not being anywhere.

A few years ago I was in Kentucky talking to my son in California. He said something about how different I sound now, more healthy. I explained that I am completely whole, completely able to be present with him, even if I am on the other side of the country. He acknowledged that he knows that to be true.

Traumatic experience needs to be acknowledged, named, identified, before it can be worked through. That is why the world does a terrible injustice to trauma sufferers by suppressing our attempts to uncover and name it. And as a whole, society suffers because of the likelihood that the trauma will get acted out in some way that is destructive.

But this is where it gets tricky. There is the reality that some people are not suppressed in their trauma story; they retell it to anyone who wants to listen. They might even embellish it, making it sound worse than it was, or even invent the story to elicit empathy or attention. People with character disorders have some twisted ways of getting their needs met.

But in my particular case, I was, and still am, suppressed by the world in my effort to uncover, understand, and heal my infant trauma. And so, I have become very adept in listening to her. The world, my world, wanted her to remain silent. By giving her a voice I am learning to speak for unborn babies in the womb and infants everywhere. They have no words and no voice, but if we listen we will hear the language of their hearts. And theirs is the very heart of wisdom and innocence.

CHAPTER FIVE
Norman
My Father

This photograph of my father was taken at the Gezira Polo Grounds in Cairo, Egypt, shortly after the raid on the oil refineries of Ploesti. He is the man on the right (as you look at the picture.)The man next to him was John Kane, the commanding officer of the 98th bombardment group.

My father is clearly in shell-shock. It breaks my heart to look at him. Notice the way the first finger on his left hand is frozen into position, cocked and ready to fire on the enemy. He was the waist gunner on the B24. His finger was no-doubt frozen into position during the entire time they made their low-altitude approach to when they crashed into the Mediterranean Sea, approximately nine hours later. Those massive bombers flew at low-altitude until they were right at the refineries, and then lifted just above what became an inferno of chaos and fire.

From an article published in 1944 in the New York Times Magazine, about my father's plane, *Hadley's Harem* titled;   *Life and Death of an American Bomber;*

"At 3:30 Sunday afternoon the formation neared the target. Ploesti is easy to recognize. It was already burning well by the pounding of the earlier waves. On the outskirts of the target's perimeter an oil storage tank spouted forth torrents of heavy black smoke, pierced by orange flames. Lindsay's voice sounded in the earphones, 'Bomb bay doors open' and Tabacoff yelled, 'One minute from target.' Then all hell broke loose." (40)

As they approached the refineries, they were only 150 feet above ground. Within minutes the plane was hit, a piece of metal was broken off the nose and lodged in the bombardier's chest, killing him instantly, his chest ripped open. My father was only a few feet away when Bud Storms was killed. At this point, one of the engines was on fire. Wind was shrieking through a hole in the nose "the size of a manhole cover." They flew on that way until they crashed violently into the Mediterranean several hours later.

My father watched as two other planes settled on the ground in the middle of the refineries, on fire. Then, as another burst into flames in the air and disappeared from sight in the instant it took to consume it and the crew. He later reported, "It was the most horrible thing I had ever seen. It is stamped on my mind."

The article goes on to describe what was going on inside the plane, the state of mind of the crew, and then the crash. "A plane hits water even harder than it hits land." The engines of the plane were on fire and ultimately died, the wind was coming through the hole in the nose, and they weren't sure that they would be landing in neutral territory. Upon impact, the escape hatch slammed shut, and the crew was trapped inside. My father and six of the other crew members managed to swim out of the sinking plane through a hole. The pilot, Gilbert Hadley, and the co-pilot, James Lindsay, were trapped inside and did not make it out alive.

If you are interested in knowing more about the raid on Ploesti, there is plenty more to read in all the accounts that have been written. For the purpose of this book, and reconstructing my father's shell-shock, I think this is enough.

He was not released from service after Ploesti. He remained in active duty, but was eventually sent back to the United States and hospitalized at a convalescent home in Florida. He was given an honorable discharge in March of 1945. By the time he returned to Warren County, Ohio, ostensibly to resume his former life, there was no life in him to do so. In a letter my aunt wrote, she says that *Norman's candle is burning low.*

After Ploesti, the family was advised that he was missing in action. During that week, they presumed he was dead. An announcement was posted in the local paper, "The combat status of Sgt. Norman Holweger, former Carlisle youth, was further complicated this week with receipt by the family of a War Department communication advising them that he had returned to active duty."

He married his fiancé, Mary Best, while he was still in service. I have been told she divorced him because of his alcoholism. He worked, or tried to work, as a mechanic at Wright Aeronautical in Ohio. He also worked as a bartender.

Then, in 1952, he married my mother, Dora Drake, a sweet young farm girl from Kentucky. The photograph taken of them while my mother was pregnant with me is the only glimpse I have of my father after the war when he felt joy. I am sure they both believed that I would be what saved him.

Earlier in this book I mention my dismay about why he did not even leave me a letter during the year he was dying. No letter telling me he loved me and hoped I would have a good life. No words written by his hand from his heart and mind. My entire life with no memories of how he sounded, or words of how he thought, or what he felt about leaving me. But I wrote that sixteen years ago when I first published this book. That was before I found his letters.

Two years ago my son told me that he had discovered on-line that my father's plane, *Hadley's*

Harem, had been brought up from the bottom of the Mediterranean Sea. You would have to understand just how frozen my mind is about my father to believe that I had not once ever thought about where the plane was, if it existed, was it at the bottom of the sea.

But I had carried the image with me my entire life of that plane. In my mother's house was a chest made of cedar. She called it a 'hope chest' for me and my sister. This was a custom then, to have a chest to keep belongings for your daughter's future. But in our hope chest, there was little more than what was left of my father's life; photographs, the flag placed over his coffin at his funeral, souvenirs from exotic places like Egypt and Africa, his medals, a string of foreign money taped end-to-end and signed by other soldiers. And, the photo of *Hadley's Harem* with my father and another crew member standing by it.

Then my son told me about the recovered plane. It would be several months before I would be able to integrate that enough to look for myself. The plane was buried in my mind, as was my father. To bring up the plane would be to bring up Norman.

On a night in July, all alone in my house in Kentucky, I made a decision to watch a World War II movie. The movie, *Shining Through,* with Michael Douglas and Melanie Griffith, was what it took to push me through being frozen about the plane. As the movie ended, I was crying so hard that my glasses steamed up, and I could hardly see the computer screen. When I typed *Hadley's Harem,* there it was, one page after another of articles about the recovery of the plane, and photographs of it on display at the Rahmi M Koc Museum in Istanbul, Turkey.

There it was, the metal coffin where three of the crew members had died, and where my poor daddy's soul was shattered forever. The plane that had been some part, big or small, in halting the Nazi war machine. The plane whose image had been in our cedar chest and then been burnt with everything else when my mother's house burnt to the ground in 1973.

There is no researcher, psychologist, student of the human mind, who can possibly understand the grief and torment I felt as I read about the plane's recovery and what happened to the crew members. All alone in my house in the middle of the night, no one to call, no daddy to comfort me because it was the daddy I was grieving for.

As I read the articles about the plane and the Ploesti mission, the other crew members aboard the *Harem* were mentioned, but still nothing about my father. Then, I opened an article written for an antique collector's magazine which began with, *There are lots of things that get stored in shoe boxes.*

The article was describing a box of letters written by a World War II soldier to family friends back home. I am thinking, *What does this have to do with Hadley's Harem?* And then, my father's name, Christopher Norman Holweger. The letters had been written by my father to family friends in Ohio. Their son Scotti was a little boy at the time, and he had been storing the letters in a box all those years.

He gave them to a friend named Eric, who later wrote the article.

I quickly sent an email to Eric, and two days later we spoke. He explained that he had eventually put the letters for sale at Ebay, but after no response, he threw them away (or so he thought.) A man named Pete called him about the letters. Eric told him the letters were gone. Pete asked him to check. Eric went out to his garage and discovered he had forgotten to throw them away. It took me a year to finally trust the letters to the mail.

Pete is the man who organized the recovery of *Hadley's Harem*, working with one of the surviving crew members, Roy Newton. Pete and I have now spent many hours on the phone. He has told me in great detail about the recovery of the plane, and all that went along with it. It is a fascinating, and horrific story. They found the skeletal remains of Gilbert Hadley and James Lindsay trapped in the cockpit. With great difficulty, the remains were brought back to the United States and those men were given military funerals.

Pete's mind is like a steel-trap when it comes to anything having to do with the Ploesti raid. He serves a sort of ancillary function for me; my brain gets so flooded when we talk about what my father and the other men went through that I can't take it in. He gives me the facts that before I was unable to integrate. My gratitude to him is boundless. Although we have not yet met in person, he is a rare and precious gift in my life. He dived to the bottom of the sea to recover my father's plane. And, our relationship has helped me to recover myself.

The days before the box of letters came to me in Kentucky, I made an altar for my father with candles and photographs. After the letters came I waited for my sister to be there with me when I opened them. There are thirty-one letters written by my father, and twenty-nine written by my Aunt Mary Holweger, who was an Army nurse.

I had no idea what a soldier during the war would write about. As we began reading the letters, I soon realized that my father's letters were under censorship. Very soon after his enlistment he was in training as a gunner. He had no idea he had been chosen for the Ploesti mission. He was probably given that knowledge only days before flying into the inferno that was Ploesti.

These letters are a miracle for me. After fifty-eight years of having no words by my father, I now have thousands. Norman is not receding further and further into some almost ancient past for me. He becomes more alive all the time. My entire life I have felt his spirit, never once believing that he had simply ceased to exist. Now I have his words, the words that came from his mind; intelligent, funny, sarcastic, boy to man in a few short months. Man who was already alcohol-dependent before he went to war. Man with such a tender heart who killed countless others from the sky.

As I have struggled to understand what we now call Post Traumatic Stress, both in my own case of trauma rooted in infancy, and also Norman's case, I realize that how combat veterans are affected by war has so much to do with who they were before they became soldiers. These letters have confirmed for me what I knew to be true of my father. Because yes, I did know him. I was his baby. I have the memory of his face embedded in my mind and heart. His eyes were so sad and brooding, his smile gentle, his arms too weak to hold me.

His mother died when he was twelve-years-old, from the tuberculosis she had suffered with for over a year. The Holweger family of Carlisle, Ohio, had their share of hardships. My father's Aunt Mamie was brutally murdered, when she was thirteen, in 1880 while walking to the country store. The newspaper did not use the word rape, but instead, outraged. There would have been a lynching if they had found the killer, but after arresting several suspects, they could not find him. This was the family farm from which my father wrote in 1933;

I feel kind of blue up here on the farm. This is the first letter in the packet I now have. It was addressed to Thel Scott, Hyde Park, Cincinnati, Ohio. We believe that Thel was a friend my Aunt Mary met in nursing school. My father may have had a boyhood infatuation with her that continued after she married and he went off to serve in the war.

On September 19th, 1942, he writes from Atlantic City, New Jersey. *Haven't been placed in any particular branch yet but am trying for gunnery.* He did in fact then become trained as a gunner.

By the end of October he was in Fort Meyers, Florida, obviously now being trained for the role as a gunner. *I'll only be here for a five week course in flexible gunnery, three of them are almost gone so in another two weeks I should be out of here. After I'm completely finished with my training I'll be sent to a pool where combat crews are formed then after a few weeks of training as a team we'll be shipped across as part of a bomb armament outfit, my part will be machine gunner. All in all about 12 to 15 weeks and I should be in the thick of it.*

November 24th, Salt Lake City, Utah. *Well after five days on a train I finally wound up out here in Salt Lake City. It seems like we gunners have to be double threat men so we have to take a six week course in radio, I think they just don't know what to do with us so they're giving us something else to do.*

Norman continued throughout the year to be trained as a waist gunner. The crew for *Hadley's Harem* was chosen and assigned the B-24 bomber, and then began the preparations for the attack on Ploesti. I do not know exactly when the crew was told they would be a part of the Ploesti raid.

On July 27th, 1943, he wrote; *Your newspaper should be full of the history we're making over here. Someday I'll be able to sit down and tell my grandchildren, bless 'em, that I was in on that show. As a matter of fact if things go as they have been I shouldn't be surprised if I'll be having that Xmas martini with you folks. Hope George had a nice fishing trip, man I sure could go for a mess of trout now. Have been swimming in the Mediterranean Sea at Bengasi but no trout."*

This one is so heartbreaking. He talks about his future grandchildren. He now has two grandchildren and six great-grandchildren. He wrote this just four days before the Ploesti raid which destroyed his life forever. He is swimming in the Mediterranean, and within days he would crash into that sea.

September 24th, 1943. *Well folks by this time you've no doubt given up on me. Tis a long story and one which I cannot write about from here. Right now I'm doing exactly nothing except waiting around trying to find out what they intend doing with the three of us. Haven't done any flying since that fateful day back in August. Had a letter from Aunt Callie and it seems like the War Dept. let the family know the worst for a few days. Hope they didn't give up too soon. I wrote and told them to put that star back in the window.*

He was declared "missing in action" for about a week. In the cedar chest which I mentioned earlier was the newspaper clipping with his photograph, *Christopher Norman Holweger, missing in action.* As with everything else about my father, the way I stored that knowledge in my early traumatized brain was that I believed he had drowned in the sea. This belief co-existed with full knowledge that he had returned home to Ohio.

I wrote this poem many years ago;

Lost at Sea
Fused together, we swam
Into that dark and raging sea
Both of us lost and drowning
Just daddy and me

She stood there on shore
Drowning too

133

Mother, my mother
Don't let this sea take you

Death and daddy whirled me 'bout
Into that dark and raging sea
Then threw me back to shore
Like used up seaweed

I lie there wrecked and broken
While he went free
Death took my daddy
And lost him at sea

The threat of total annihilation is a deep and enduring thing within me. My father's fear of annihilation became my own. The arms that should have been strong and steady enough to hold his baby instead flailed about in water believing he was drowning in the sea. Flashbacks totally obliterate the present moment. All the moments of my infancy when I should have felt security I instead felt fear and a turning inward upon myself, knowing that I should not have been brought into the world; his world.

And what are my symptoms related to infant traumatic stress? The same as every other PTSD sufferer, plus a few that are more idiosyncratic to me. I already explained my terror upon waking from afternoon naps.

Then there is the fact that it is very difficult for me to record images of faces. My brain simply can't remember a face until I have seen the person a few times. Once, I had gone on a date with a man who I liked and hoped I would see again. By the next morning, his image was gone. When I tried to recall it, I could see his body and the clothes he was wearing, and his hair. But where his face should have been was blocked out, like if you are watching something on television and the face of the person is screened out to protect their anonymity. Explain that one fellow researchers.

For as long as I can remember, since I was a very young girl, I have had a sense of a foreshortened future. This is now considered one of the hallmarks of PTSD, especially with young children who have witnessed death. I simply do not believe I will be alive a few months from the present moment, going back for over 40 years. I did not believe in solidifying my career because I didn't think I would be around to have one. I didn't buy a house because I wouldn't be here, and so I am still renting. If someone says something to me about a future date, like let's get together in six months, I think to myself *Don't they know I will be dead by then?*

"The last avoidance criterion for PTSD, C7, is identified as a sense of a "foreshortened future." This symptom means that the person feels as though his or her expected course of lifespan development will be truncated, short-lived, or profoundly altered in uncertain and anxiety-provoking ways. The spector of a sense of foreshortened future may lead to an urgency to live life fully in the present and consequently to engage in risk-taking and acting-out behaviors. When a strong sense of foreshortened future predominates the individual's future orientation and planning, the immediacy of the present is overvalued. The result is psychological myopia in which tomorrow may never exist in the eyes of the person." (41)

I also have a distortion of chronological age. I have always felt much older than my age. In the photograph of me taken a few weeks after my father's death, my eyes look so old and sad. I am still an infant but because of the suffering I had witnessed I was already wise, the sort of wisdom that is born of suffering. For example; in my thirties I would not date a man more than a year younger than myself because I felt I was too old for him. This distortion is not easy to explain. Essentially, my own age has never had any relevance to me, it's always been just a number.

My "present is overvalued." Each and every instant, each and every encounter, seems to hold a life-altering significance to me. I am one of the most driven people I have ever known. Unfortunately I have driven myself right to the "poor house." Many of my nightly-dreams involve being in vehicles, losing vehicles, not being able to find the keys to a vehicle. The vehicle is always felt as a symbol for the need to get someplace with a total sense of urgency.

And all these symptoms I have just described are delineated in the language of behavioral psychology. I report that I have an on-going belief that I will not be alive a few months from now, and that this belief has persisted for over forty years. The evidence for this can be seen in my life; I haven't bought a house and don't make long-range plans. This is also corroborated by other PTSD sufferers who report the same symptom.

But how do we even begin to explain the biology of it? It is not simply a belief, something I persist in telling myself. Belief is defined as an acceptance that something is real and true. So is my belief that I will die within a few months an irrational belief? The belief has persisted for many years. Rationally speaking, I am not yet dead and so therefore it seems to be a false belief. But the reality is that we will all die, and at the age of sixty I am growing closer to my own death. Therefore, the belief becomes more rational with each passing moment.

Biologically, how did this belief get encoded into the structures and chemistry of my particular brain? How does it persist over time? How is it that being with a dying father for the first year of my life, and then watching his very dead body being carried out in a body bag, get translated deep into my brain (encoded) as a belief that I myself will soon die?

What is common to all organisms is that there is some internal form of communication going on. Of course, this internal communication system is the most complex in humans. Because external communication with other organisms reflects the internal system, human beings also have the most complex system of communication with our fellows. To understand this, we have to shift to a more neurobiological approach and language.

"Communication is what neurobiology is all about. The modes of communication include membrane conductances, patterns of neuronal spikes and graded potentials, electrical and chemical transmission of synapses, secretion, and modification of neural function." (42)

These internal systems can be studied in animal research and then translated into models for the study of humans. It appears that the animals most often used are rats, rabbits, and primates. The animals are researched using various stress experiments: footshock, swimming for long periods to avoid drowning, deprivation of stimulus, noise, extreme temperatures, and chemical exposures. From these experiments researchers then measure levels of stress-related hormones and neurotransmitters. Since these substances are also a part human brain chemistry it can then be inferred that the same mechanisms are involved when humans are exposed to stress.

In an article titled *Role of Amygdala in the Coordination of Behavioral, Neuroendocrine, and Prefrontal Cortical Monomine Responses to Psychological Stress in the Rat,* the authors demonstrate that being exposed to stress activates dopamine, serotonin, and norepinephrine metabolism in the anteromedial prefrontal cortex. They then translate what relevance these results might have to human behavior and pathology; 'These results are discussed in terms of possible relevance to stress-induced exacerbation of schizophrenic symptoms and the pathophysiology of post-traumatic stress disorder." (43)

I am opposed to animal experimentation for the understanding and treatment of human disorders. We have enough information now that has been gleaned through the suffering of animals. Why are we not being smarter in using this to be a more sane humanity?

The very definition of sanity is to accurately perceive reality. If I believe a bear is chasing me and there is no bear, that is either delusion or hallucination. If an anorexic looks in the mirror and sees fat on her legs when she is a day away from dying of starvation, that is also delusion. If a therapist tries to argue someone out of the belief that she will be dead in a few weeks, instead of investigating the very deep encoding that has happened in her brain, then that therapist is only doing more damage.

We can work with clients in a way that affirms their inner reality, while gently challenging unreal beliefs. But this is where it gets sticky. One of the criteria in the Diagnostic and Statistical Manual (DSM) for schizophrenia is religiosity. Therefore, if I as a Christian woman talk to a non-Christian therapist about the reality of Christ and the Holy Spirit, that therapist then sees my belief as delusion.

What is needed is a far deeper understanding of all that makes us human. During the years I worked in psychiatric treatment, many of my schizophrenic patients complained of auditory stimuli; they heard things in their head when there was apparently no external source to explain this. I never tried to argue them out of it. Instead, I tried to understand the nature of these voices. Some patients report that they are picking up radio transmissions... who is to say they aren't? Some believed they were hearing the voice of God... I myself have "heard" the voice of God.

My most important function with those patients was to witness their very real suffering. We had a female patient in her thirties whose diagnosis was Borderline Personality Disorder. One day she ran out the back door, obviously agitated. I found her sitting on the stairs, crying and looking like she was in hell. She jabbed at the scars on her arms where she had been cutting herself over the years.

"Look, look at my arms. My pain is real."

I gently touched the scars and told her that I knew her pain was real. She then relaxed as we sat together in silence on the steps.

Emotional pain is every bit as real as physical pain. It does not go away just because you tell someone they shouldn't have it. If we see it as a sign of deeper processes in the mind and heart, then, and only then, can we use it to lead us to real insight.

The emotional pain connected with early trauma is particularly persistent because of what it taps into. When our core relationships caused us pain, shame, and terror, our sense of being forever unsafe is real. When we are the victim of the evil that exists in the human world, we can never truly reclaim innocence. That doesn't mean we can't find any peace and joy, but it is not an innocent peace, it is a peace with full-knowledge of evil and suffering. It is a wise and enlightened peace. It is sanity.

Norman did not recover from the Ploesti mission. He suffered continually for the remaining ten years of his life. Because he is not here to understand his own shell-shock, I will, for the remainder of my life, try to understand it for him.

Colonel John Kane, commanding officer of the 98th Bombardment Group of B-24 Liberators (my father's unit) wrote this in his war diary; it is a fitting epitaph for Sergeant Christopher Norman Holweger;

"I must say 'So long' to each of those brave warriors who did not complete their last mission, still flying out there in the Blue. To you men who fly on forever I send that part of me which cannot be separated and is bound to you for all time; I send to you those of our hopes and dreams that never quite came true, the joyous laughter and showery tears of our boyhood, the marvelous mysteries of our adolescence, the glorious strength and tragic illusions of our young manhood, all these that were and perhaps would have been, I leave in your care, out there in the Blue. Keep up your airspeed; and don't break a wing; hold her steady out there. One of these days, I will take off to join you. When I do, I hope you will teach the Old Man how to fly."

CHAPTER SIX
Dora
My Mother

My mother was born in 1930 in Hazard, Kentucky, to poor and uneducated parents. Southeastern Kentucky, was, and still is, one of the most impoverished regions of the United States. She weighed a little over two pounds. She was born in a farmhouse, and her family carried her around in a dresser drawer lined with a blanket for fear of holding her. She survived.

A few years before her passing seven years ago, I started being more curious about how her incredibly low birth weight had affected her mental development. I had done so much of my "daddy work" but who was my mother and what was my "mommy work" to be?

Because she was such an innocent and I was still not whole nor skillful enough to examine this with her, I never once discussed any of this with her. Early on in my process about her I asked to have this revealed to me in dreams. Right away I had a dream. We were helping to deliver a baby. The umbilical cord needed to be cut. My mother held the scissors with a shaking right hand, while her other hand held a lit cigarette. She was totally not present, looking away from the baby as she started to cut the cord. I took the scissors from her.

When she died seven years ago, it was from lung cancer that had spread to her liver. I knew that she had been a smoker since she was very young. But I never once asked her if she and my father smoked in that one-room apartment where I had suffered such neglect and trauma. I assume they did. Everyone was smoking in rooms with children then.

As I began investigating this issue of her extremely low birth weight, I read somewhere that one of the last structures in the brain to develop is the corpus callosum, the bundle of tissue that connects the right and left hemisphere of the brain. I contacted an association formed by people who themselves had suffered a failed corpus callosum development, or had a family member who had. When I explained my mother's symptoms that indicated inadequate mental development, it fit exactly with what others were reporting.

The National Organization of Disorders of the Corpus Callosum cites a study done of individuals with the disorder. They were shown photographs of emotionally intense social scenes, and then measured for galvanic skin response and heart and respiration rate. The results "suggest that although the right hemisphere is capable of triggering an appropriate psycho-physiological emotional response the lack of communication between the left and right hemispheres prevents patients from expressing these emotions in the ratings."

This fits so exactly with who my mother was. Until I began studying the findings regarding agenisis (complete or partial absence) of the corpus callosum, I did not have the language of science to describe what I had observed in my mother. Before that, I would describe it as my mother's lack of emotional response unless things got really bad, and then you could almost see her trying to turn her brain on. I was always aware that she was a better father than she was a mother in that she worked hard for a living and provided a stable home for us, but when it came to the nurturing or emotional insight we expect from a mother, it took deliberate effort on her part to summons that in herself. I have no memory from my childhood of my mother ever holding me, saying she loved me, or giving me emotional comfort. Not because she was hard-hearted, but because she did not have that sort of brain capacity.

The one and only time I ever heard my mother express any awareness about her own mental limitations was in the admitting room of the hospital, a few days before her death. The nurse asked what grade she had completed in school. She replied the 8th grade and very respectfully asked the nurse why they needed that. The nurse replied it would help them know how to explain medical procedures to her. And then she made some comment (I forget what exactly) that indicated that she knew her brain did not work in the same way as other people.

While she was still alive, I asked her older sister, my Aunt Ruth, if she had ever thought my mother's brain had not developed right because of her being a two-pound baby. She told me of an incident when they had been out walking with my grandma. My mother was about ten and walking ahead of them. Ruth asked their mother if she thought my mom walked a little funny because of being born too soon, and grandma replied yes.

My mother had rheumatoid disease for the last twenty-five years of her life and became very crippled. At one point, she had surgery to remove all the bones in her toes and replace them with metal pins. So any gait problems were masked by then.

This photograph was taken of her when she was about ten-years-old. My mother is the blond girl standing in front. You can see that her left foot is turned inward, and that she is not looking at the camera the way the other girls are, as though she is off in her own world somewhere. My Aunt Rosaleen stands behind her.

A failed corpus callosum development prevents abstract reasoning (being able to interpret the

146

more complex reasoning that is crucial to human relationships.) One example is this; on my children's birthdays, she would always send them a card, and it always had a one dollar bill in it. When they were six they thought that was great, not so much at sixteen. My mom had not embraced the concept of inflation. When she was sixteen a dollar would have been a fortune. She could not comprehend a more appropriate way to let them know she was thinking of them on their birthday.

She was unable to pick up on social clues. She would tell an off-color sexually suggestive joke at a family gathering in the midst of our Puritan-like female relatives. The men would laugh and the women would be embarrassed for her. She held a second-class position within her own family.

If we were out in public, she often stared at other people, in the way a small child does. We would have to say to her that it wasn't polite to stare at people that way.

Now that you have a better idea of her, you can make some sense out of my earlier comment that her reply to my question about how my father could lift me out of the crib after his surgery when he had been told to lift nothing heavier than a pencil, was "I really don't know."

Dora was the most pure, self-sacrificing, and loving woman I have ever known. She never met a person she didn't like. Her unconditional love for me sustained me throughout my life. But that love was evidenced by her actions, never by saying the words. She was always there, cooking for us, going to work, laughing at my jokes. But when I say *my mother wasn't all there* I mean she literally was not all there; some part of her brain never developed.

She was not able to give me any meaningful advice in most situations. My pain was always invisible to her, and so after my miscarriage at fifteen she never once mentioned it again. Not because she was cruel or judgmental, but because it would have required a more abstract sort of reasoning to comprehend all that the miscarriage implied.

As I began to understand the full reality of my mother's mental limitations, I could then begin to understand my infant and child self in relation to the other who she was.

D.W. Winnicott refers to the mirroring role in the mother (and father) child relationship;

"This to which I have referred in terms of the mother's role of giving back to the baby the baby's own self continues to have importance in terms of the child and the family." (44)

Given that an infant's self is given back to it by the primary caretakers, particularly the mother whose womb it has emerged from, what was the self I was given back from the parents I have just described here, Norman and Dora? The father with severe shell-shock, dying from some combination of neuropsychiatric and physical injuries and alcoholism, and the mother with severe mental and maternal limitations, living in constant dread of losing her husband.

I was given a self permeated with and imprinted by constant threat and insecurity, a self who did not have any sense of its own continued survival, a self who came to see human relationships as fraught with pain and danger, a self who at her very core was sad and fragile. And I am still that self. My wholeness comes from the work I have done to realize that I was made by the very stuff of my parents, and that, knowing this, I am not at war with myself any longer.

Allan Schore writes;

"Furthermore, the mother is not only acting as a modulator of the child's current affective state, she is also regulating the infant's production of neuro-hormones and hormones which influence the activation of gene-action systems that program the structural growth of brain regions that are essential to the future socioemotional development of the child." (45)

The socio-emotional legacy left to me by my father was PTSD. What my mother left me was an almost non-existent ability to feel anything. As a child and young woman, I simply did not experience much joy, anger, excitement, embarrassment, connectedness, or aliveness. This isn't to say there weren't deeply programmed feeling states of fear or shame. But those states push us away from human relationship, not towards it.

My mother is no longer here for anyone to examine her brain functioning. Fetal brain development is so very complex, and has everything to do with connectivity. The corpus callosum is the largest connective structure in the brain, estimated to have 190 million axons which transfer information across the two hemispheres.

Agenesis of the corpus callosum means complete or partial failure of its development.

I will never know if my mother's corpus callosum was affected by her low birth weight and premature birth. Or what other structures in her brain were underdeveloped. Now, years after her passing, to try and investigate this fills me with sadness. To look at photographs of two-pound babies breaks my heart for the little being who grew up to become my mother.

But it is impossible to piece together all the pieces of who we are without looking at our relationship with our mother. This is also true for anyone who was given up by their mothers. We were in their wombs. It was our first home. We were impacted by that relationship, it formed us, it has a deep-reaching effect on us for the rest of our lives. If we had a healthy beginning with our mother, then we began life given what we needed to thrive and grow up whole. But, if we were not, the missing pieces of that relationship need to be examined.

My mother's mother, my grandma Ila, was so dear to me. She was the adult in my life who I felt the closest to. She passed away when I was twenty-four. But as I have come to know her nine children over the years I understand just how inadequate she was as their mother. She was self-centered, incapable of nurturing them, and lacked insight. What was her relationship to her two-pound baby, my mother, like? Probably almost non-existent.

Look at some photographs of two-pound babies. A neonate who is that tiny and underdeveloped looks like it needs to be put back inside somebody's womb. It does not elicit the same response in us as a well-formed newborn with its sweet face and perfect hands and feet. It instead looks foreign and unlovable. My tiny little mother would have seemed like a thing in a drawer to her own mother, I am certain of it.

The one and only time I ever heard my mother cry was at my grandma's funeral. My mother, who never expressed strong emotion, wailed with her grief, something wrenched from deep inside her for the mother who was lost to her forever.

Although she was named Dora for her mother's mother, no one ever called her that. Her nickname was Bobbie Jo. The reason for this was that her two older sisters, who took care of her, had boyfriends at the time named Bobbie and Joe. This somehow to me has always seemed an indicator of her own maternal deprivation. Everyone else but my grandma supplied the nurturing and care she needed to survive.

I worked through much of my pain and guilt about my mother in one of my historical novels. I have written and published eight novels set in Kentucky in the 1800's. This one is titled *Caledonia*. Two sisters, Callie and Mary, were born at Fort Boonesborough. Callie's relationship to her younger sister Mary is really my relationship to my mother. As I crafted Mary's character, it was my mother who I drew from. This is one of the scenes;

"Mary had been born the year before their father died. That winter there was a starving time at the fort and the baby had been affected while still in

Laura's womb. She had seemed fine for the first three years of her life and everyone would comment on what a beautiful child she was. Her hazel eyes looked out upon her world with such innocence and peace. But it became obvious that she had not been born quite right. She walked with a slightly unbalanced gait and had trouble finding words when she needed them. She had continued to grow physically and had turned into a stunningly beautiful young woman. She was now nineteen and Callie was twenty-two. They were inseparable.

Mary, because of her limitations mentally, was so very hurtful sometimes. She said exactly what came to her head. Yesterday she had told Callie that the dress she was wearing did not become her because she was too flat on top. Laura had chastised her, with more intensity than usual.

"Mary, don't you know that is a hurtful thing to say to someone?" She was clearly angry with her youngest child woman.

Mary's face took on the look of a playful puppy that has been disciplined for something it can't comprehend.

"I'm sorry Callie. You know I would never hurt you."

Laura was not done with her. "Can't you understand that makin' a comment to another woman about bein' too flat would hurt her?"

"But why mama? It's just the truth."

"What is the truth Mary?"

"Men like women with big bosoms, like mine. If Callie wore dresses with lower necks she wouldn't look so flat."

Callie had sat up straighter in her chair to remind herself that she wasn't quite as flat as the picture her sister was painting. She exchanged a look with Laura that held little comfort. She could see that their mother was also weary from the type of mothering a daughter like Mary required.

"Mary, I want you to start thinkin' about the things you say before they come flyin' out of your mouth."

"Think about them? Well, what would I think mama?"

When my mother died, I was stricken with grief. But there was another emotion which is not so easy to admit to. I felt relief. A lifetime of being her protector, of suppressing my own self, of knowing all the pain and hardship of her life even more deeply than she herself could feel it, was over.

She was so crippled by the rheumatoid disease by the end of her life, but refused to use a walker or cane. She hobbled about, never complaining, always serving others. On her tombstone we engraved this epitaph;

She faltered by the wayside and the angels took her home.

May you rest in peace my dear sweet mother. You gave us all you had to give. No, it was not enough for me to grow up well and whole. But it was plenty enough for me to know I am loved.

CHAPTER SEVEN
Light Within Darkness

There is no coming to consciousness
without pain. People will do anything,
no matter how absurd, in order to
avoid facing their own Soul.
One does not become enlightened
by imagining figures of light,
but by making the darkness
conscious.

CARL GUSTAV JUNG

Carl Jung was born in Switzerland in 1875. He was a psychiatrist, and a contemporary of Freud and the other psychoanalysts. He initially supported Freud, and they had a major influence on one another. Jung developed his own theories and methods of practice, calling his work Analytical Psychology, which developed over time into Jungian Psychoanalysis.

It was Jung, more than any of the others, who brought the spiritual dimension into psychological work. Most students of Jung know this. But few people probably realize just how profoundly Jung affected the movement known as 12-step fellowship, begun by Bill Wilson from a need to conquer his own alcohol dependency. From those first seeds has grown an international movement with groups spanning a broad spectrum of human addiction and dysfunction. When I was very deeply involved in my own 12-step work, I realized what a miracle the program is.

Jung had a patient, known as Rowland H, who was also working with Bill Wilson. In 1961, Jung and Wilson exchanged letters regarding the influence Jung's work had on Rowland, and ultimately the direction the entire 12-step process took by acknowledging the necessity for a relationship with God (or a higher power.)

Wilson wrote to Jung;

"I doubt if you are aware that a certain conversation you once had with one of your patients, a Mr. Rowland H. back in the early 1930's, did play a critical role in the founding of our Fellowship."

In this very long letter, Wilson goes on to share his spiritual conversion, influenced by Jung's work with Rowland;

"In utter despair I cried out 'If there be a God, will he show himself?' Then immediately came to me an illumination of enormous impact and dimension. If each suffererer were to carry the news of the scientific hopelessness of alcoholism to each new prospect, he might lay every newcomer wide open to a transforming spiritual experience. This concept proved to be the foundation of such success as Alcoholic Anonymous has since achieved."

Jung then wrote to Wilson, regarding the work he had done with Rowland while he was his patient;

"His craving for alcohol was the equivalent on a low level of the spiritual thirst of our being for wholeness, expressed in mediaeval language: the union with God... I am strongly convinced that the evil principle prevailing in this world, leads the unrecognized spiritual need into perdition, if it is not counteracted either by real religious insight or by the protective wall of human community... You see, Alcohol in Latin is 'spiritus' and you use the same word for the highest religious experience as well as for the most depraving poison. The helpful formula therefore is: spiritus contra spiritum."

He closed with the 42nd Psalm;

"As the heart panteth after the water brooks, so panteth my soul after thee, O God."

Our work is to make conscious the darkness, seek the light, and to realize that claiming who we are, and what our world is; both darkness and light, safety and danger, good and evil; is where wholeness lies. And, fundamentally, it is a work we do with God, in whatever way we can concede to the realm of spirit.

Safety; meaning comfort, order, positive feelings, security, always feeling good and never bad, and freedom from pain and fear. But this is not the constant state of being human, is it? The attachment to all this can be as much of a trap as the dangers.

Ideally, we should know the greatest safety and security at the very beginning of our lives. But this was certainly not true in my case. There was danger, from the beginning. Because of this I have become a familiar to the darkness, not denying that it exists in the world, but always attempting to understand and decipher its code so that I can be free of avoiding it or seeking it, or avoiding or seeking the safety. This, to me, is enlightenment.

Modern life is filled with challenges and obstacles to safety which we have named depression, anxiety, shame, and rage. The level of severity of these emotional states is directly connected to the severity of trauma we have suffered. All emotional states, arise from, and contribute to chemistry, in the brain and body. The cause of depression might be drug-induced, genetic, or grief about losing someone. But, in each case levels of neurotransmitters will reflect the same changes.

Instead of denying the negative we can work with it in such a way that it begins to lose power over our lives. The more our knowledge of all that has shaped us deepens and grows, the more able we are to look at ourselves in a way that is both more clinical (observing our own symptoms) and at the same time more compassionate. If I am having a really bad day, I do not chastise myself for having a really bad day.

Being in a deep depression is like walking through life in molasses. Even the most simple tasks, like buying groceries or getting dressed, becomes overwhelming. When we are depressed it isn't just that we feel sadness and hopelessness, but our bodily functions are more depressed. Our mind seems to barely be able to process information and movement seems slow and unnatural. If we are in what is called an "agitated depression" we might be moving very quickly but the underlying feeling is depression.

For myself, when those times come, I have learned to just surrender; and when I surrender, I surrender to my God. My soul is the clay in the Potter's hands; the work that is being done at the deepest level of who I am is beyond my understanding in those moments.

If we have bouts of suicidal thoughts, or attempts (obviously if the attempt was successful you wouldn't be reading this book) we can begin to observe ourselves in a way that is both more objective and more compassionate. When I am dealing with a client who expresses suicidal feelings, I will suggest this to them; imagine that the part of you that feels like committing suicide is simply a part that really does need to die so that the rest of who you are can have a chance to live. It is the part of you that feels so much pain it can't live anymore; but, it isn't all of who you are. Think about someone you know who doesn't feel so much despair. What is it that makes them so different from you? Can you begin to imagine your own life in such a way that allows for the pain to loosen its grip? And if there is something you have done that causes so much guilt, shame, or anxiety, that you don't see how it can get fixed, step back some from it. Look at your life as a powerful river that carried you along a certain course. Who you truly are, your true self, is not that river.

If there is a situation you're in that you feel is not reconcilable, can you begin to see that it may be you who is telling yourself it can't be fixed, or altered in some way? Once, when I was feeling hopeless about a situation I was in, someone gave me this advice. She said, "Pretend it is someone you love who is going through this, and then sit down and write them a letter about what you think they should do."

I went home and wrote the letter, pretending it was my daughter who had grown up and was facing the situation. I immediately knew what advice to give her.

On the other hand, to say that all that we experience in life is what we tell ourselves about it is false. Certainly, physical pain, disability, how we look, and past events, are real. Not everything in life is reconcilable. But knowing that, having someone like me say that for you, helps to alleviate the power it has over our lives. We can suffer, and suffer fully, and still make the choice to go on living.

So much of the pain we feel in life has to do with the very sticky business of human relationships. The opposite of feeling pain (and other negative states) is what we call sociopathy; a sociopath does not feel pain in human relationships. They are operating on a different system. For the rest of us (which is most of humanity) we navigate through life by emotions derived from our relationships. We feel guilt (pain) because we have hurt someone; we feel joy and satisfaction when we get positive feedback from someone we admire. This is what socialization is, and it begins in our infancy.

This feedback system is very much a part of the cultural and political context in which we live. What is condoned and admired in one group, may be punished in another. Individuation is about separating ourselves out from the others enough to become who we are.

One of my client's in a diversion program for teens, who had been cited for drug and alcohol use, was needing help with individuation. In my private session with his parents they were concerned because he had become very depressed that year. They told me they knew that if they took him to a therapist the recommendation would most likely be to put him on medication. I told them that I am not an advocate for using medication to treat depression, and I would meet with their son to see what I could discover. I will call him Steve.

Steve and I met in my office. It was apparent right away that he was very intelligent, and had a good and stable home. When questioned about the depression, he told me that he felt different than the other teens around him because they were all in total support of the invasion against Iraq that had recently occurred, and he saw the political situation that had developed very differently than they did. He had become increasingly shut down because there was no one he felt he could talk to about what he really believed.

So, we talked, and in me he saw that there are people who shared his views. He lightened up, he laughed. I witnessed his mind come back to life. I called his father after the session and said that I believed Steve would come out of the depression if he could more openly share his thoughts with others who were open to what he needed to say. The next week his parents expressed their gratitude to me for giving their sweet and intelligent boy a chance to be heard. Then, one day as school let out I drove by Steve, walking hand-in-hand with a young woman. He was smiling, she was looking at him with adoration as he looked toward the sky, busy expostulating on some idea or other. Isn't such young love born of two minds and hearts that find each other and soar into the heavens together?

There is probably no one who would have recommended that I deal with my anxiety and depression in the way I have over the last thirty years. Therefore, I am not recommending that you deal with your anxiety and depression in this way either.

High anxiety states tax our hearts and central nervous systems by over-producing stress hormones. Chronic anxiety causes us to age prematurely and makes it difficult to function well. Besides, people won't want to be around us much if our anxiety is out of control.

Those who knew me before I had the breakdown thought of me as being very calm. I was calm, and I was repressed and dissociated. There was almost no feeling happening in me; not emotionally, not physically. The years prior to the breakdown, I was in a marriage to a man who was a "dry alcoholic." I was having fits of rage towards him, but other than that I was pretty much a walking dead woman.

When the panic attacks came, I made a conscious choice to not suppress, or even ameliorate, them. I sensed that the anxiety was what would be needed to propel me through the wall of denial the world had erected around my infancy.

And I was right. Everywhere I have turned, people have refused to see the value or credibility of trying to heal infant trauma. I hurled myself against those walls and I was anything but calm while I was doing it. It was as though I had an anxiety gage and I would allow it to rise just enough to break through the denial, and then turn it down just a notch. In some strange way that I don't quite understand, anxiety became my defense against the world's denial. I am feeling calmer now, but not much.

I had done enough meditation practice to know that I could attain a deep sense of inner peace and equanimity with it. But, I asked myself, how would that be different from medicating it? I could try to medicate it away, or meditate it away. I realize that this analogy will be unacceptable for many people. They will reason that of course the state you reach with meditation isn't the same as taking a tranquilizer. In most respects, it isn't the same. But, after a lifetime of being dissociated, it seemed to me that reaching a state of detachment through meditation was just too close to what I had been and what kept me from getting in touch with my inner infant, the one who was so traumatized.

I needed to let her feel the anxiety, and the grief, and the rage, that the world denied her. Now I have started meditating again.

What I am suggesting is that we don't have to run from the anxiety. We can let it come up and then look at it some. What can it teach us? What triggers it? What caused it in the first place? For those of us suffering with Post Traumatic Stress Disorder, anxiety can be used in a way that is life-enhancing.

When we are threatened we can flee, fight, or freeze. In my case, I was pretty much held captive in a crib for the first year of my life watching my father try to drink away the horror he had suffered in the war. And then, early one morning he bled to death on the floor and they took him away forever. What did I go through?

There was no way for me to fight, there was no way to flee. Instead, I became a frozen little baby girl in a crib. It wasn't until my breakdown at the age of forty that I got unfrozen.

Learn to work with your anxiety. Learn the ways to turn it down a notch or two when you need to. But don't be afraid of it. Exercise, diet, yoga, meditation, medication, massage, and just plain ol' having fun are all good ways to ameliorate anxiety.

Anger is a healthy response that lets us know when something is hurting us or someone else. As children, our natural anger is so often suppressed that it gets very bottled up inside. Anger that is not allowed some form of expression gets compounded and becomes rage. By this I am not suggesting that children need to be overindulged in their self-expression. There is a very big difference between

164

a child who has a legitimate reason to be angry, and a child who is spoiled.

Both men and women need to seek a balance in our anger responses. With men, because of the high level of testosterone, rage often becomes a force that is damaging to them and everyone around them. Aggression is such an on-going reality for males that society has institutionalized its expression through sports, and unfortunately, through war.

Young boys receive incredibly conflicting messages about their anger. They learn that it is not okay to murder your next-door neighbor, but that if you put on a uniform and then commit murder, you will be a hero.

Girls, on the other hand, grow up with the message that young ladies do not show anger. We become conditioned very early to always be nice and conciliatory. Then, once we put our foot upon a spiritual path, we are told we should not feel anger and should forgive those who have hurt us. As a Christian woman, I have struggled with the rightful expression of anger. Jesus was angry with the money-lenders when he threw them out of the temple. Mahatma Ghandi taught that we should be angry at the issue and not the person. This to me has been a very helpful approach.

Many years ago, my sister and I were almost in what would have surely been a fatal car crash. I was driving and we had just left our mother's house. We came around a curve and a car was passing a truck and coming straight at us head-on going about 40 miles an hour. I swerved off to the shoulder and the other driver lost control, flipped over a guardrail, and turned his car upside down. By the time we got to him he was on his hands and knees and had blood all over his back. He had been drinking whiskey all morning and was drunk out of his mind.

I lost control. I jumped up and down and yelled at him over and over, "I'm not mad at you . . . I'm mad at you being drunk and almost killing me and my sister". When he was released from jail two days later, I went and found him and berated him some more. But the whole time I had love for him in my heart.

If we can find the appropriate place for anger in our lives it doesn't then fester and turn into rage. If we were terribly hurt in childhood then we may need to connect with the anger that we weren't allowed to have then. If there was a perpetrator who abused us, then it may be necessary for us to work with our anger towards them.

Because my trauma wasn't due to abuse but instead was caused by the reality of war neurosis and death, I have had a very hard time my entire life being able to experience anger. The first time I ever gave expression to my rage was when I was married to an alcoholic. The rage that welled up inside me then was so engulfing that it nearly destroyed me.

I am learning now how to channel my anger in a way that benefits me and the world I live in. There is so much that we should be angry with. If we can begin to identify what, or who, we are really angry with, then we can work toward positive change.

Shortly after I began uncovering the trauma I shared with my father I came across a photograph of myself taken within a few months after I watched him die. As I attempted to uncover and heal the "daddy" wound I so often felt at odds with everyone. It just seemed like no one recognized the importance of what I had committed myself to. So, I stopped looking to others for approval. Instead, whenever I felt confused about which way to go, I would look at that baby picture and ask her, "What should I do?"

And she would tell me what to do. Sometimes she would 'say' (meaning my inner self informing me) "Can we just lay down and take a nap?" or "Could you stop going around so-and-so; they aren't good for us." I learned to trust the innate wisdom inside myself who is that baby girl.

Do that for yourself. Remember who you were back then, find a photograph if you can, and ask that baby girl or boy (or boy/girl) what it is you need to do. Not abandoning ourselves is often a hard habit to form. We have had so much practice with self-abandonment.

The more you practice being there for yourself, the more you will understand what I mean. When that negative committee in your head starts blaming and judging you, just tell it to be quiet. Then, acknowledge yourself for what you're doing right and remind yourself about what's not working.

What we call "mirroring" in psychology is a crucial function supplied by the adults in an infant and child's life. And, most of us did not get healthy and balanced mirroring from our environment. We didn't get it because our caretaker's didn't get it.

Mirroring means reflecting back to a child who and what they are, in a sane way. A child does a drawing of a bird, or does something nice for a sibling; then it should be "Good job... I saw you do that nice thing."

But caretakers who are healthy need to also reflect back what needs to be corrected; "That wasn't okay to cut up the birthday cake before everyone got here. Now, go to your room and think about it for fifteen minutes."

As an adult, you need to supply the mirroring for yourself. Just as though you are your own child; when you do something good and right, acknowledge yourself. And when you do something not-so-nice, take yourself to task about it. Do your work about it and then move on.

Begin the investigation into your own life. I feel so strongly about this because the investigative work I had to do was primarily of my infancy. Since I could not readily pull up conscious memories, I had to go on a fact-finding mission. The people who are our elders, who were there to witness our prenatal and early childhood, will pass away some day. It is important to find out all you can from them. If they are like my family, they will be resistive and behave as though you have no right to know. Ignore that and keep digging.

As I started to collect more data about my own infancy, the deep grief that had been with me for forty years began to resonate with the facts. That's when I knew that I had connected with the real me, the one who was so wounded. This is what I call reconstruction.

Learn to have boundaries and let others have theirs. Establishing appropriate, but flexible, boundaries is a key task in healing. This means identifying what you are comfortable with and what you're not. What is your physical and emotional comfort zone? How can you tell when your boundary is being violated and then how do you let someone know that in a way that is appropriate to the situation?

Because we did not learn to have boundaries before, we have to learn now. Like any other kind of learning, it takes practice. As I have worked with having appropriate boundaries, there have been many times I have erred too far in one direction or the other. For those of us whose boundaries were severely violated as children, this process can be excruciatingly painful and can bring up reservoirs of toxic shame that we didn't even know we had.

Several years ago I attended a performance and art exhibit by incest survivors. The trauma we witnessed that night being voiced in the form of spoken-word was extreme. Afterwards, we all sat in a circle and shared our feelings about the event. I said that although I am not an incest survivor, my earliest memories are sexual, involving sex-play with other girls.

After the group, a woman approached me, certain I am sure of my denial. She asked if maybe I just wasn't aware of having been incested by my father. I explained that I have done so much work around my early life, and that I feel fairly certain I was not an incest victim. I believe that my father's physical relationship with me was not inappropriate; it was just so all-encompassing that when it was gone, nothing else mattered but getting it back.

If I met that woman today, I would give another answer. The truth is, I am an emotional incest survivor. The first time I heard the term "emotional incest" it hit me in such a powerful way; I knew it is true for me. What this means is that the adults in your life did not adequately respond to your emotional and mental developmental needs; but instead, used you to meet theirs.

Imagine a terminally ill man suffering with shell-shock, taking care of his baby daughter every day for a year. The ego goes through a dissolution in death. Everything that he held on to in life was breaking away; leaving only death. Those long hours alone with me, his deepest emotions poured into this child he was leaving behind. Such terror and grief I must have taken in from him so he wouldn't feel so alone. Because we lived in a one-room apartment, I would have witnessed whatever sexual activity he engaged in, either by himself, or with my mother.

The ego boundaries, and physical boundaries, I should have been developing, were obliterated with his dying. Boundaries enable us to know what is inside us, and what is outside us. On a physical level, it means differentiating what is outside our own skin. On an emotional level, it means differentiating what is outside our own head. I was emotionally incested by my father and mother.

Understanding this has been an important key in unlocking the door of who I am.

The healthier we become the more flexible our boundaries will be. Once we know what they are we don't have to be quite so rigid with them. In the early stages of recovery people can be very uptight and inflexible about boundary setting. I was once at a 12- step meeting and when I went to shake a man's hand at the end of the meeting, he jerked his hand away and quickly explained that he couldn't even have that much contact with a woman because it "triggered his sexual addiction."

Another time, a woman set some boundary with me. I think it had to do with not calling her at home. I felt so deeply shamed and angry with her. Then, I gave myself a good talking-to. I realized that if I wanted others to honor my boundaries then I needed to honor theirs, and that she was also learning how to do it right. When others set boundaries with us, it isn't about us. It's about them reclaiming their own sense of self. This is how we all get healthier together in our global community.

Find balance in your life. When we are trying to heal, life can feel like a pendulum swinging out of control. We fall in love, get our hearts broken, and then swear off relationships forever. We go on a fad diet, and then lose control and binge for the week-end. We refuse to spend money even on necessities, and then go on a wild shopping spree.

Our brain, in its natural, healthy state, seeks homeostasis (the tendency toward a relatively stable equilibrium between interdependent elements, especially as maintained by physiological processes.)

Neurotransmitters have an optimum level for balanced functioning. It's not as though some are good and some bad. When we engage in unbalanced behavior we throw our brain chemistry out of sync. Our brain becomes a pendulum swinging back and forth inside our head causing disruption to all aspects of our lives.

This is why addiction is so damaging. It takes us further and further off-center. We live in an addicted, out-of-control society. We are continually bombarded with manipulation to buy more, use more, waste more. More, more, more. But, the outcome is then less, less, less. More spending creates less money in our bank account. More eating unhealthy foods creates less blood sugar a few hours later. More sexual addiction creates less self-esteem and healthy relationships.

Healing is about balance. It is about using activities and substances in a way that supports homeostasis. There are some activities and substances that have no place in a balanced life. Physical violence and methamphetamines serve no one. Assertiveness and a little caffeine might. As we work with this idea of balance we each find what works for us. Our pendulum begins to gently swing back to center.

Give back more than you take. Healing isn't just about getting; it's also about giving. There is no satisfaction that equals serving others and serving our planet and her creatures. We are all interdependent. When the very capacity to love and serve is destroyed, that person is then sociopathic; without a conscience. And these are the people who do the most devastating damage to those around them. Adolf Hitler was sociopathic.

What I take, I have to give back, so that the cycle of life can be continually renewed. You may not choose to grow your own food, but the next person you smile at on the street may then do something nice for someone who is growing the food you eat. We can stop being continually preoccupied with our own needs and comfort.

Recently, I went to a reconciliation service at a Catholic Church. Reconciliation is the act of being reconciled with God. We were instructed to write on a piece of paper all that was keeping us from a closer relationship with God. At that time, my anxiety about making a living was so high I could hardly even breathe, and that is what I wrote on my piece of paper. When I met with the priest he instructed me to go home that evening and make a list of my blessings. The list I made went on for two pages. I saw that I had become so obsessed with getting more that I had failed to stop and give thanks for all I had been given.

This is one of the reasons that support groups are so important for healing work. When we are in groups we immediately get to see how coming out of ourselves serves others. The more we give in the group the more we get back. There have been many times that I have experienced someone in a group saying that they had heard someone say something in a previous group that had helped them so much along the way. And, sometimes it has been me that they are talking about.

I feel so blessed that my commitment to healing is being sent out into the world like ripples on a pond. I witness others coming out of themselves and see how this is what reconnects us to humanity.

Being human can be so very lonely. Loneliness isn't cured by living in close proximity to others. There are plenty of people living lives of quiet desperation in crowded cites. But there are also people who isolate in rural areas. What cures loneliness is knowing that we are a vital part of the world around us.

If you are feeling cut off, then find a way to give something back. Volunteer at a nursing home, find a pen pal in a third world country and send them a few dollars that you were only going to waste anyway, get politically involved, start a community garden. When we get stuck in pain and rage it stifles our natural generosity. Be there with the pain when you need to, but then when you're having a good day, give something back.

Addiction can be seen as a quest for wholeness, a longing and an insistence on something deeper, more true and powerful. Ultimately we realize that our method of realizing all of that is not found in addictive substances and activities. We then keep moving forward through the darkness into light. We shed off a false self and claim the true self we were meant for. We achieve union with our own Soul and with God.

My infant self was brought too close to the horror of Nazi Germany and the world war by my year with my father. She knew darkness. My work as an adult has been to listen to her, to study the war in all its intricacies, to understand what her brain was made of, and to help her reclaim the relationship with the father who is always just there on the other side of the door.

And by doing all this, I led her back to the light she was truly meant for.

EPILOGUE

Sometimes now I can almost imagine what a healed world might be like. Before I started my own healing journey, I had no such hopes or imaginings.

And even now, with people the world-over in such turmoil and dire conditions, I find myself at times feeling hopeless about it. Everywhere we turn we see destruction to the environment and human life. Healing can seem so impossible that we choose to just stay shut down and in denial.

A healed world can only be made from healed people. Thomas Merton wrote; "If the citizens are sane, the city will be sane." Healing doesn't mean that we find a cure for all of life's problems. We never will. But what would it be like if all of those problems which are inevitable in life; natural disasters, death, illness, old age, loss . . . were responded to with love instead of violence? What if compassion could replace fear?

Coming out of denial about my own trauma eventually led to coming out of denial about the world's trauma. It has been very hard to integrate it all and not feel despair. There is a balance we need to find and it is this balance that will allow us to be sane and whole.

We need to not be in too much denial, but we also need to not be so engulfed by the fear and evil that it destroys us. We need to balance the hard work of healing with nurturing our capacity for joy. It is there, in the center of all that, where we can rest for a moment and find a self that knows peace and wholeness.

In the twenty years that I have worked as a counselor, I have had several hundred clients and patients. Every single one of them has inspired me to believe in the profound human capacity for healing, even in the face of incredible trauma and tragedy. I wish you could have been there with me sitting in my seat as I witnessed and was a part of the shifts that took place in those hearts and minds.

When I worked in the methadone clinic, I hung a painting of a rose on the wall behind the chair where my clients sat. As they were speaking, I would see the rose behind them, and be reminded that each client had a place inside of them just like the rose; a place of beauty and perfection.

That office, along with every other office and group room I worked out of, was filled with many tears and lots of laughter. As I am finishing this book, I am flooded with the faces and stories of all the men, women and teens who have opened up their souls to me. I can't imagine that I would have had the courage and wisdom to do my own healing had I not known them.

Those clients are societies cast-offs. They live out their days in psychiatric hospitals, drug and alcohol treatment programs, prisons, and jails. The teens were in diversion programs due to committing felonies or abusing alcohol and drugs. They were all human beings who found themselves in a fast-moving river that swept them out of the way of ordinary life without ever having a chance to heal. They are each a sad indictment of just how inadequate our systems are in bringing about true healing. All of us together can keep working toward a more free and just world.

In 1699, John Locke wrote, "The little and almost insensible impressions in our tender infancies have very important and lasting consequences and there 'tis, as in the fountains of some rivers, where a gentle application of the hand turns the flexible waters in channels that make them take quite contrary courses; and by this direction given them at first in the sources they receive different tendencies and arrive at last at very remote and distant places."

Let us all work to bring back from those remote and distant places all of those who got carried away beyond the hope of healing graces.

BIBLIOGROPHY

Life and Death of an American Bomber; by C.L. Sulzderger. The New York Times Magazine, 1944 (1, 40)

Inside the Brain; by Ronald Kotoluk. Andrews & McMeel Publishing, 1996 (2 , 14)

If Someone Speaks, It Gets Lighter; Dreams and the Reconstruction of Infant Trauma; by Lynda Share. The Analytic Press, 1994 (3)

Characterological Transformation; the Hard Work Miracle; by Stephen M Johnson. W.W. Norton & Company, 1985 (4, 21, 24, 25)

The Psychopathology of Everyday Life; by Sigmund Freud. W.W. Norton & Company, Inc. 1965 (5)

The Invention of Memory; by Israel Rosenfield. Basic Books, Inc. 1988 (6, 7)

The Myth of Repressed Memory; by Elizabeth Loftus. St. Martin's Press, 1994 (8)

Waking the Tiger; by Peter Levine. North Atlantic Books, 1997 (9)

Banished Knowledge; Facing Childhood Injuries; by Alice Miller. First Anchor Books, 1991 (10, 11)

Mein Kampf; Adolf Hitler (11)

Drama of the Gifted Child; by Alice Miller. Basic Books, 1994 (12)

For Your Own Good; Hidden Cruelty in Child-Rearing and the Roots of Violence; by Alice Miller. Farrar, Straus, Giroux 1983 (13)

Trauma and Recovery; by Judith Lewis Herman, Basic Books, 1992 (15)

Attachment and Loss, Volume 1; by John Bowlby. Basic Books, 1969 (16, 17)

In Search of the Real Self; by James F. Masterson. Collier MacMillian,1988 (18)

Anaclitic Depression in an Infant Raised in an Institution; by Robert N. Emde, Paul Polak, Rene Spitz. 1965 (19)

Affect Dysregulation and Disorders of the Self; by Allan N. Schore. W.W. Norton and Company, 2003 (20, 21, 28, 30, 45)

The Psychological Birth of the Human Infant: Symbiosis and Individuation; by Margaret S Mahler. Basic Books, 1975 (22)

Healing the Shame That Binds You; John Bradshaw. Health Communications, 1988 (26, 27)

Life Before Birth; the Challenges of Fetal Development; by Peter W. Nathanielsz. W.H. Freeman and Company, 1996 (29)

Molecules of Emotion; by Candace Pert. Simon & Schuster, 1997 (31, 32)

Test Reveals Brain Network Responsible for Involuntary Flashbacks; by Ralph Heussner, 2010 (32)

Women Who Run With the Wolves; by Clarissa Pinkola Estes. Ballantine Books, 1992 (33)

Introduction to Neurobiology; by Heinrich Reichert. Oxford University Press, 1992 (34)

Can Adverse Neonatal Experiences Alter Brain Development and Subsequent Behavior?; by KJS Anand and Frank M Scalzo. Published in Biology of the Neonate, 2000 (35)

The Trauma of War; Stress and Recovery in Vietnam Veterans; American Psychiatric Publications, 1990 (36 & 37)

Review of Awakening the Dreamer: Clinical Journeys by Philip M Bromberg; by Allan Schore 2007 (38)

Neurobiology and Treatment of Traumatic Dissociation; Towards an Embodied Self; by Ulrich F

Lanius, Frank M Corrigan, Sandra L Paulsen. Springer Publishing, 2014 (39)

Assessing Psychological Trauma and PTSD; edited by John Preston Wilson, Terence Martin Keene. Guilford Press, 2004 (41)

Comparative Neurobiology; by C Ladd Prosser. John Wiley & Sons, 1985 (42)

Role of the Amygdala in the Coordination of Behavioral, Neuroendicrine, and Prefrontal Cortical Monamine Responses to Psychological Stress in the Rat; by Lee E Goldstein et al; published in The Journal of Neuroscience, 1996 (43)

Playing and Reality; by D. W. Winnicott. Tavistock Publications, 1971 (44)